ON BECOMING A COGNITIVE BEHAVIORAL PSYCHOTHERAPIST

Cognitive behavioral psychotherapy is much more than a series of skills and techniques, but rather a vital human activity. It starts with the inner being of the therapist, that is, his or her personality and character, and then moves to the outer world of strategies and tactics. Drawing on a wealth of personal and professional experience, Dr. Russell Grieger illuminates ten inner perspectives that transform a technician into a psychotherapist, including the fundamental nature of being human, the power of passionate purpose, fearlessness, the pursuit of elegance, ridding self-esteem, and more. For the practicing clinician, the therapist in training, and the interested layperson, this book should be in everyone's library.

Russell Grieger, Ph.D., is a licensed clinical psychologist with more than thirty-five years' experience of treating individuals, couples, and families with Rational Emotive Behavior Therapy. He is also an Organizational Consultant and an Adjunct Professor at the University of Virginia.

Also by Russell Grieger

Handbook of Rational-Emotive Therapy: Volume I (with Albert Ellis)

Cognition and Emotional Disturbance (with Ingrid Grieger)

Rational-Emotive Therapy: A Skills-Based Approach (with John Boyd)

Handbook of Rational-Emotive Therapy: Volume II (with Albert Ellis)

The Rational Emotive Therapy Companion: A Clear, Concise, and Comprehensive Guide for the RET Client (with Paul Woods)

Fearless Job Hunting: Powerful Psychological Strategies for Getting the Job You Want (with Bill Knaus, Sam Klarreich, and Nancy Knaus)

The Undefeated Season: The Newspaper Story of the 1964–1965 Evansville College Purple Aces Basketball Team (with Tom Tuley)

The Couples Therapy Companion: A Cognitive Behavior Workbook

Developing Unrelenting Drive, Dedication, and Determination

ON BECOMING A COGNITIVE BEHAVIORAL PSYCHOTHERAPIST

Russell Grieger, Ph.D.

NEW YORK AND LONDON

First published 2018
by Routledge
711 Third Avenue, New York, NY 10017

and by Routledge
2 Park Square, Milton Park, Abingdon, Oxon, OX14 4RN

Routledge is an imprint of the Taylor & Francis Group, an informa business

© 2018 Russell Grieger

The right of Russell Grieger to be identified as the author of this work has been asserted by him in accordance with sections 77 and 78 of the Copyright, Designs and Patents Act 1988.

All rights reserved. No part of this book may be reprinted or reproduced or utilised in any form or by any electronic, mechanical, or other means, now known or hereafter invented, including photocopying and recording, or in any information storage or retrieval system, without permission in writing from the publishers.

Trademark notice: Product or corporate names may be trademarks or registered trademarks, and are used only for identification and explanation without intent to infringe.

Library of Congress Cataloging-in-Publication Data
Names: Grieger, Russell, author.
Title: On becoming a cognitive behavioral psychotherapist / Russell Grieger.
Description: New York : Routledge, 2018.
Identifiers: LCCN 2017039929 | ISBN 9781138229044 (hardcover : alk. paper) |
ISBN 9781138229051 (pbk. : alk. paper) | ISBN 9781315390444 (e-book)
Subjects: | MESH: Psychotherapy, Rational-Emotive–methods | Professional
Autonomy | Self Concept | Personal Narratives
Classification: LCC RC480.5 | NLM WM 420.5.P8 |
DDC 616.89/14–dc23
LC record available at https://lccn.loc.gov/2017039929

ISBN: 978-1-138-22904-4 (hbk)
ISBN: 978-1-138-22905-1 (pbk)
ISBN: 978-1-315-39044-4 (ebk)

Typeset in Baskerville
by Deanta Global Publishing Services, Chennai, India

To all my mentors,
who taught me
everything I know
and use,
and
especially to
Albert Ellis, a genius,
who enriched my life
beyond measure.

AUTHOR'S NOTE

All names and identifying data/characterizations, except those of my own family, have been changed, all to protect the privacy of the people in this book.

CONTENTS

Acknowledgments	xi
About the Author	xiii
Preface	xv

1. The Nature of Being Human: The nexus around which all therapeutic decisions need to be made — 1

2. The Power of Passionate Purpose: The fuel that stimulates sustained high energy, enthusiasm, and satisfaction — 25

3. Fearlessness: The courage to do what is needed — 45

4. Interpersonal Intelligence: Building the trust and goodwill needed to bring about quality change — 57

5. Destroy Self-Esteem: Self-esteem is the problem, not the solution — 75

6. Unconditional Personal Responsibility: The root source of extraordinary performance and results — 91

7. Psychological Freedom: From misery, indecision, compulsions, and addictions — 107

8. The Pursuit of Elegance: Beyond feeling better to getting better — 123

9 Make War on Perfection: Be perfectly imperfect 137

10 Happiness on Purpose: If it's going to be, it's up to me 155

Epilogue 169

Index *171*

ACKNOWLEDGMENTS

Any book—whether it be personal, professional, or fictional—is the product of a lifetime of experience. How could this one be an exception? So many people, too many to name, have had an input in this one.

I must first thank all of the patients who have entrusted their happiness and well-being into my hands. It has been my honor to have served them, and I offer to them my deepest gratitude. I have gained as much or more from them as they have hopefully gotten from me.

I am deeply indebted to my writing teacher, editor, and friend, Jay Kauffmann. Jay has taught me that writing can be more than just a professional activity, but a personal passion as well. He not only helped me express myself better, sentence by sentence, but he pushed me to go deeper, further, bolder into the experiences that are at the heart of this book. He made me sound like myself, only better.

As always, I owe so much to my wife, Patti. She typed every word, on every page, not once, but through many rewrites. Not only that, but she made cogent suggestions throughout, always making the text better than when she first picked it up. Always an angel, never failing to be supportive and encouraging, she was more so than ever on this project. How lucky can one guy be?

How can you thank someone when thanks are never enough? A genius, a man of vision, a bold heart, Albert Ellis revolutionized psychotherapy, thereby benefiting millions of people throughout the world. I count myself as one of them—both personally and professionally. I feel extraordinarily fortunate to have known him and to have been so impacted by his wisdom.

ABOUT THE AUTHOR

A recognized leader in the theory and practice of Rational Emotive Behavior Therapy (REBT), Russell Grieger, Ph.D., is a licensed clinical psychologist with more than thirty-five years' experience helping individuals, couples, and families overcome their personal problems and lead happy, fulfilled lives. At the Albert Ellis Institute in New York City, he has held the status of Fellow and Training Faculty Member, served on the International Standards and Training Committee, and edited the *Journal of Rational Emotive and Cognitive Behavior Therapy*. He currently is a member of the Editorial Board of the Albert Ellis Tribute Book Series.

Dr. Grieger also provides consultation and training to organizations big and small, public and private, with the purpose of helping them fulfill their mission and reach their potential for high performance. He focuses on leadership development, teambuilding, managing change, strategic planning, building motivation, conflict resolution, high-powered sales, and emotional well-being in the workplace. He has been a pioneer in developing methods to enhance an organization's culture of commitment, discipline, and personal responsibility, as well as in helping those in leadership roles develop the inner qualities of character and personality that lead to extraordinary performance and results.

ABOUT THE AUTHOR

Russ received his undergraduate degree from the University of Evansville, where he played on two consecutive NCAA Championship basketball teams, and his Masters and Doctoral degrees from The Ohio State University. An Adjunct Professor at the University of Virginia, he has authored eight professional books, over seventy-five chapters and articles, a series of self-help audio cassettes, two recent books for the layperson—*The Couples Therapy Companion* and *Developing Unrelenting Drive, Dedication, and Determination*—and a memoir, *The Perfect Season*. He lives with his wife and son in both Charlottesville, Virginia, and St. Thomas in the U.S. Virgin Islands.

PREFACE

It was late spring, 1970. I stood at the twenty-yard line of Ohio Stadium, the football home of The Ohio State Buckeyes. Shaped like a giant horseshoe, the two-tiered concrete colossus dwarfed the graduation ceremony which had just ended. I looked up to the top rows and located my reserved seat, tucked between two massive turrets, a giant scarlet and gray Ohio State University flag flapping back and forth on each. The thought crossed my mind that I must look just as small from up there as did the players I saw on Saturday afternoons.

But I didn't feel small, not that day. Clutching my tasseled cap in one hand and my Ph.D. diploma in the other, I glanced toward the far end zone and impulsively assumed the Heisman Trophy posture, cradling an imaginary pigskin tight to my chest, and laughed out loud.

Regretfully, my high spirits didn't last. Four months later, I found myself behind a battered wooden lectern, delivering my first professorial lecture as a twenty-eight-year-old Assistant Professor at the University of Virginia. Before me sat twenty graduate students, most just a few years younger than me, some older. Their notebooks opened, pencils poised, they stared at me expressionless.

Until that moment, I assumed I would glide seamlessly from graduate student to university professor. For five years, I had taken the classes, studied the books, absorbed the knowledge of one clinical supervisor after another. But, standing there, beneath what felt like a spotlight, I realized the absurdity of my position, how limited were my experiences, how shallow my insights. If not a sham, I was certainly a novice. All I knew was to forge ahead, feign confidence, and pretend I knew more than I did.

But I persevered, balancing teaching with treating a few patients until I resigned to start a full-time psychotherapy practice almost a decade later. Over the years, I have mastered Rational Emotive Behavior Therapy, successfully treated countless patients suffering from nearly every mental malady in the diagnostic manual, and confronted more clinical challenges than I can count.

Only now, after decades of sifting through, around, and behind the countless conversations I have had with my patients, do I feel capable of teaching that first course. But it would surely not be the one I taught then, one exclusively focused on tools, strategies, and skills, as if the human relationship called psychotherapy could be reduced to a cookbook of recipes.

Today, I'd sit with my students around a large rectangular table. Naturally, I'd teach them the basic theory and practice of Rational Emotive Behavior Therapy. But I'd emphasize that the source of therapeutic excellence does not come from what is written in textbooks or spoken in lecture halls. It comes from the wisdom gained from years of providing psychotherapy to patients suffering from problems of practically every shape and substance. I'd teach them what I've learned after thirty-five years of clinical practice, including the following:

- **The Nature of Being Human**, the core feature that all humans share, upon which all psychotherapeutic decisions must be based.
- **The Power of Passionate Purpose**, the creation of which gives meaning to each day's efforts, sparks unrelenting drive,

and provides pleasure, pride, and satisfaction, for both the therapist and the patient.
- **Fearlessness**, meaning the courage to make the tough decisions, to risk resentment and even rejection, to accept the fact that not everyone will appreciate you or your effort.
- **Interpersonal Intelligence**, which includes people skills, but also the deep paradigms and principles that spawn the unconditional acceptance, generosity, and compassion each patient wants and deserves.
- **Destroy Self-Esteem**, a concept alien to most psychotherapists, but a condition essential to mental health and deserving of promotion in psychotherapy.
- **Unconditional Personal Responsibility**, the key to taking charge of one's emotions and actions, refusing to fall into a victim mentality, and doing what it takes to create a life one loves to live.
- **Psychological Freedom**, the ultimate goal of all psychotherapy, to free the patient from the root source of all the emotional contaminants that blocks one's ability to fulfill deeply cherished dreams and desire.
- **The Pursuit of Elegance**, that is, finding elegant solutions to people's problems, solutions that bring about deep personality change rather than mere symptomatic relief.
- **Make War on Perfectionism**, in all its shapes and forms—perfect approval, perfect performance, perfect fairness, perfect comfort and ease.
- **Happiness on Purpose**, the goal which all humans desire and perhaps the ultimate goal of psychotherapy as well.

These topics comprise the contents of *On Becoming a Cognitive Behavioral Psychotherapist*. To my clinical colleagues, I recognize that there are many stepping-stones to effective psychotherapy and these are but some. But, I assert that they can elevate a clinician from a mere technician into a psychotherapist. To you non-clinicians, I not only hope that you find intriguing what's in these pages, but also bits of enlightenment that will help each of your days be happy, healthy, and productive.

Russell Grieger, Ph.D.
Clinical Psychologist
Charlottesville, Virginia
June, 2017

1
THE NATURE OF BEING HUMAN
The nexus around which all therapeutic decisions need to be made

*The happiness of your life
depends on the quality of your thoughts:
therefore, guard accordingly and
take care that you entertain no notions
unsuitable to virtue and reasonable nature.*
– Marcus Aurelius

Well into January of 1973, the middle of my third year on faculty at the University of Virginia, I sat in my cubbyhole of an office. It felt cramped, though it contained only a dwarf-sized desk, a narrow two-shelf bookcase, and a collapsible metal chair. Three small windows near the ceiling kept the room from feeling totally claustrophobic.

Heretofore I felt I belonged in such a setting. Undistinguished and untenured, I worried that I would morph into my undergraduate psychology professor whom I had come to disdain. Of medium height, an inch or two of belly hanging over his belt, and sporting a garland of gray hair that started at one ear and circled the back of his head to the other, he'd stand behind a thick wooden podium and spout practically word for word what was written in the text. No amount of tonal inflection, hand gesturing, or pregnant pauses could hide the fact that the only thing that separated him from us was that he had read the text before we had.

But gradually things had begun to change. For the past year I had treated a handful of patients under supervision to fulfill the requirements for my clinical psychology license. There was the middle-aged divorcee, bitter and despondent over her failed marriage; the graduate student experiencing severe anxiety about completing his doctoral dissertation; the promiscuous thirty-something who connected her self-worth to the attention of men. These cases, plus a few more, began to form my professional identity, gave me the sense that I was, in fact, an honest-to-goodness real psychologist.

On that January day, I sat hunched over my desk, my lecture notes scattered in front of me, laboring to enrich my presentation with gems from my patients' stories. I was so engrossed in my prep work that I jumped when the phone rang. On the line was Laura, one of the four new clinicians hired by the University of Virginia's Student Counseling Center. She requested that I supervise her and her colleagues so they could meet one of their conditions for their licensure as clinical psychologists. In an instant, I felt the weight of expectation, wondering if, with my limited experience, I could be of any real help.

We sat weekly at the Counseling Center on facing velour couches that felt like they swallowed us when we sat down. With the overhead fluorescent lights switched off, the dim glow from lamps on the four end tables created a cozy, intimate atmosphere. The only thing missing was Eagles' music and cocktails.

The format never varied. My colleagues took turns presenting a patient—the referral complaint, the symptomology and background data, hypotheses about etiology, and proposed treatment strategies. Then the rest of us would weigh in with our feedback and suggestions.

I found it intriguing that each of my colleagues paid allegiance to a theoretical orientation that mirrored their appearance and temperament. Laura could have matriculated right out of Freud's parlor in Vienna, what with her blouse always buttoned tight at her neck and her way of observing without revealing much of what she thought. Gary, bespectacled, slight of stature, and soft-spoken, had adopted the non-directive approach of Dr. Carl Rogers. Billie stood tall and slender, with the taut body of an Olympic sprinter. Wearing her Afro tight to her head, accentuating her chiseled cheekbones and straightforward no-nonsense delivery, she practiced behavior modification right out of B. F. Skinner's school of operant conditioning.

Beth proved to be the exception. Slightly overweight, she secured her black hair atop her head with pins that failed to prevent strands from falling over her eyes and scattered her notes about her which she picked up and discarded in frantic bursts. Her presentation consisted of a hodgepodge of techniques with no discernible system of psychotherapy to guide her choices. She workshopped a freshman who suffered from test anxiety and proposed a list of coping devices—deep breathing, physical exercise, talking to a friend. She told us about a third-year student who was depressed over a break-up with his girlfriend. Her interventions included a quick return to dating, a focus on his good qualities, and offering him unconditional acceptance. Then she shared the case of a graduate student who was guilt-ridden over a recent abortion. Her proposed tactics were to encourage her to keep busy, seek the support of other women who had undergone the same procedure, and engage in positive affirmations.

The group labored to deepen Beth's work, offering her strategies that might help her penetrate further into her patients' psyches. As we struggled, I started to feel uneasy, knowing that there was something missing, that Beth needed more from us than new and better techniques. But what?

Then I got it. It wasn't more techniques that Beth needed. She needed a solid grounding in the core nature of what it means to be human, a conceptual model that would guide her to an intelligent choice of techniques to use with her patients. Without this, I realized, she would never be more than a mental mechanic, fixing a gasket here, changing a spark plug there. And that's what I said, careful to make my point in such a general way that Beth wouldn't perceive herself to be singled out.

The room fell silent, except for the ticking of the wall clock. Everyone stared at me. Before I could figure out what to say, Beth jumped in. "That makes a lot of sense to me."

"To me, too," I said, realizing for the first time that what I had just said applied as much to myself as it did to her.

The truth was that my own theoretical grounding was in its infancy. I had been introduced to the theory and practice of Rational Emotive Behavior Therapy (REBT)[1] by one of my professors at Ohio State over schooners of Budweiser at an off-campus neighborhood bar. At first I scoffed at how superficial and simplistic it sounded. But, at his insistence, I read several of the seminal books written by REBT's founder, Dr. Albert Ellis—*How to Live with a Neurotic* (1957), *Reason and Emotion in Psychotherapy* (1962), *A Guide to Rational Living* (1967). I found the assertions he made about the mechanics of human emotional disturbance and its cure straightforward, logical, and persuasive. They avoided the obscurity and mysticism of many other therapies.

That meeting at the Counseling Center stimulated me to deepen my understanding of REBT. As a first step, I attended a one-day REBT seminar delivered by Albert Ellis at the annual American Psychological Association's convention in Washington, D.C. When I walked into the conference room, I found the three hundred or so seats mostly filled, except for one right of center in the first row. I settled in and studied Dr. Ellis. He sat slouched behind a wooden table on a slightly elevated platform, munching a tuna sandwich, apparently indifferent to the packed room before him. He was dressed in an open-necked shirt, rumpled slacks, and scuffed shoes, all apparently worn more for comfort than style. He had a thin, wiry body; a long, angular face; and a prominent nose atop which rested black horn-rimmed glasses. *Woody Allen*, I thought.

But he didn't come across nebbish-like when he spoke. His voice seemed to penetrate directly to the brain. Without hesitating or halting, he gestured with his bony hands and peppered his remarks with off-color words. The longer he talked, the larger he seemed to grow until, after a while, he seemed to permeate the room with his brilliance.

Dr. Ellis spent the morning laying out REBT's ABC model of human emotional disturbance and its process of psychotherapy. Then, in the afternoon, I watched him bring the words to life. With volunteer patients from the audience, he crawled inside REBT and deftly got to the core of these people's troubles. What struck me was the straightforward way he led the conversations, without frills or hesitation, direct and to the point.

Joyce[2] volunteered first. She wore jeans and a black crewneck sweater. With her black hair cut short and framing a rounded ivory-complexioned face, she fidgeted while waiting for Dr. Ellis to begin. Then he quieted the audience and got right down to REBT.

"So, Joyce, what problem would you like to start with? Something you're troubled about."

"I have a lot of troubled feelings about my relationship with my mother," she said, without hesitation.

"Is this all the time or when she's doing something?"

"Well, she lives far away, so it's mostly when we're on the phone."

"But, when you say troubled, let's break it down. Is it anger? Depression? What is the troubled feeling?"

"Mostly anger," Joyce said, clearing her throat.

"I can hear that in your voice," Dr. Ellis said, smiling at her for the first time. "Could you give a recent example when you were on the phone and got angry with her?"

I concentrated almost exclusively on Dr. Ellis during this exchange. From my angle, over Joyce's shoulder, I had the sensation of looking directly into his eyes as if I were the patient. I felt the intensity of his focus, the power of his commitment to fixing Joyce's problem.

Joyce went on to tell a long story of her mother interrupting her evening paperwork with a phone call and carrying on about trying to get her younger sister back into the religious fold. She concluded, "I said to her, 'Mom, why can't you just let her alone, accept her the way she is?' My mother started yelling and I started yelling and I hung up on her." As she progressed through her story, her hand gestures increased and her neck reddened.

"So," Dr. Ellis said, "sometimes your mother gets after your sister to do what she wants her to do—religion or anything else. Then, when you hear that, you feel angry. Now, let me ask you: at that point, what do you think you're saying to yourself about your mother to make yourself angry? Because we control our feelings by our thoughts and thereby make ourselves angry. What do you think goes on in your head while your mother is doing this?"

"She's butting in where it's none of her business."

"That's right," Dr. Ellis said, leaning forward and pointing to his temple. "But there is more in your mind, isn't there? Aren't you first telling yourself something rational and then following that with something irrational? You're first saying to yourself, 'She's butting in and I don't like it.' If you followed that with, 'but that's just my mom, she's human, so what,' you'd let it roll off your back. But, instead, you're adding the irrational thought, 'Because I don't like it, she shouldn't do it.' Right?"

"Hmmm."

"I want you to see that it's not your mom that's causing you to be angry, it's your damning her for not acting the way you want.

To let go of your anger, you've got to give up that kind of thinking toward her. Do you see that?"

"Uh-huh."

There it is, I spit out under my breath. I had just watched Albert Ellis directly and swiftly pinpoint Joyce's anger problem. He had acted out what I had only read in his books about what makes people tick.

First, it is not what happens in people's lives that cause them to react as they do. Rather, it is the way they think about what happens that prompts their responses. Ellis puts this into a simple ABC model in which A stands for the Activating Event (in this case, Joyce's mother's annoying behavior), B is the Belief about the A ("She shouldn't act this way!"), and C represents the Emotional and Behavioral Consequences of the Belief (Joyce's anger).

Second, disturbed people hold both rational and irrational beliefs. Like their more healthy brethren, they hold the desire to do well, to be liked and approved of, to be treated respectfully and fairly, and to get what they want in life. Then, when thwarted at A (the Activating Event), like Joyce with her mother, they react appropriately with such feelings at C (the Emotional Consequences) as frustration, irritation, sadness, disappointment, and/or regret. But, unlike their more healthy brethren, they have also learned to perfectionistically demand that they do well and receive approval, be treated the way they want, and be provided a satisfying life. They thereby cause themselves to overreact with depression, anxiety, guilt, or, as in Joyce's case, anger.

Third, no matter where, when, or how a person learned their irrational, disturbance-producing beliefs, that person is disturbed today because he or she still endorses those beliefs as God's gospel truth in the here-and-now. While tracking down their early history may be dramatic and interesting, it is for the most part unnecessary.

Then Ellis continued with Joyce.

"Okay, Joyce, if you want to let go of your anger toward your mother, you've got to get that kind of thinking out of your head. You'd better show yourself, over and over, why it's irrational, and then repeatedly convince yourself with more rational thoughts. So, think about it: why is it irrational to demand that your mother not act as she does?"

Joyce tilted her head, considering, then said, "Well, because she's human."

"Exactly!" Dr. Ellis said, his voice raised and emphatic. "She's a fallible human being, who isn't perfect and never will be. She must have faults. Furthermore, she must have the faults she has, not the ones you give her permission to have. You're demanding that, because you don't like her faults, she shouldn't have them."

"Pretty arrogant of me, I guess."

"Be careful not to use the same perfectionistic demands on yourself as you do on your mother, Joyce. Being imperfect, you too must act badly at times, but don't damn yourself for it. Now, what's a more rational way to think that won't lead to you getting angry at your mother?"

"Like you said earlier," Joyce said, "I don't like it when she acts like that, but she's a fallible human."

"That's right. Now, if you practice that daily for the next one hundred days or so, especially when your mother calls, the chances are you'll habituate this rational way of thinking. Then you'll mostly, but not perfectly, get rid of your anger. Will you commit to doing that?"

"I will."

"Okay. Best of luck to you," Dr. Ellis said, extending his hand and smiling, "and thanks for volunteering today."

With that brief exchange I witnessed the best of what Albert Ellis had to offer. He pointedly demonstrated the fourth and fifth key provision of REBT:

Fourth, it's the job of the REBT therapist to be active, involved, and directive with the patient. This means that he or she takes an authoritative stand in teaching the ABC model, encouraging self-responsibility for causing one's own emotional disturbance, helping the person ferret out the disturbance-producing beliefs, showing how to use the logico-empirical method to dispute these irrational beliefs, and helping to re-indoctrinate more rational beliefs that will lead to responding appropriately. The therapist teaches, teaches, teaches.

Fifth, to bring about significant personal change, the patient must work long, hard, and repeatedly to bring about the cognitive restructuring that will lead to symptomatic relief and the desired emotional state. There is no short cut or easy, quick fix.

Sitting in this D.C. conference room, watching Albert Ellis work his magic on Joyce, and then three more volunteer patients, I felt energized. The brilliance of the theory and practice of REBT became clearer and clearer to me. As the afternoon progressed, a sense of authenticity spread through me. *That's it,* I thought, *the center of being human is the deeply endorsed beliefs people hold—about themselves, other people, the world.* I couldn't wait to get back home to my own patients and apply all this.

Spurred by my newfound zeal, I devoted myself throughout the rest of the nineteen-seventies to mastering REBT. I devoured every REBT book in print, listened to countless audio tapes of Albert Ellis demonstrating REBT, and attended as many REBT training programs at the Institute for Rational Emotive Behavior Therapy in New York City as my schedule permitted. I realized that only with a clear understanding of the core nature of being human could I make the right decisions for those who put their health and happiness into my care.

The final stage of my clinical identity started in December of 1980, on a cold, gray day between Christmas and New Year's Eve that was to deliver eight inches of snow before nightfall. I resigned my tenured Associate Professor position at the University of Virginia and stepped into the life of a full-time clinical practitioner. Not only did I now live the professional life I had always dreamed about, but the number of patients I treated mounted into the hundreds through the early nineteen-eighties. While some proved simple and others challenging, all were instructive.

There was, for example, thirty-seven-year-old Shirley, housebound for the previous three years after recovering the repressed memory of a rape enacted upon her in her early twenties. Her conviction that it would be unbearable to ever be so violated again created such anxiety in her that she refused to leave the safety of her home. Then there was forty-five-year-old Brian, a transplanted New Yorker suffering from the psychotic belief that his uncle had cheated him out of his inheritance of over ninety percent of Manhattan's real estate. As I suspected, he refused to relinquish this delusion, but I was able to free him of his virulent damning of his uncle, which fueled his obsessive search for justice. And then there was the twenty-two-year-old anorexic college coed named Rachel, who had just been released from the hospital because of severe malnutrition. Her eating disorder stemmed from the conviction that her worth as a human being depended entirely on having the perfect body.

These patients taught me so much. Gradually I came to suspect that REBT's ABCs might be too linear, lacking in complexity and context. I came to believe that what was needed was a more complex, dynamic, and three-dimensional model—a model that could more accurately capture the intricacies of the human mind.

In a paper I published in 1985,[3] I tried to describe the complexities of the B in the ABC model, the role of B in creating a person's perception of reality at A, and the power of the individual to even create the Activating Event (the A's) independent of any environmental change. It represented my own REBT version of the fundamental nature of being human. What follows are its five components.

1. The Primacy of Thinking

To understand the nature of being human, we have to begin with the proposition that human beings are complex, multi-modal creatures who independently and transactionally sense, desire, emote, behave, and think. They share the first four of these attributes with many other creatures. But the fifth, the capacity to think, is, as far as we know, unique to humans, in at least two regards.

First of all, humans are so thrown to think that they find it virtually impossible to not think. I demonstrate this in seminars by having participants relax and close their eyes. Then I tell them, "When I say 'go,' you are to stop thinking for one whole minute. Don't think at all. But if a thought does cross your mind, any thought at all, raise your hand and keep it raised. Be sure to keep your eyes closed until I tell you to open them."

Then I say, "Okay, ready, set, go."

Within seconds, one, two, then three hands raise. Pretty soon, all of them are in the air. Barely fifteen seconds has elapsed.

"All right, everybody," I say, "keep your hand raised and open your eyes."

They look around, then burst into laughter, seeing that everyone has raised their hands.

"What'd I tell you," I say, smiling. "It took just a few seconds for all of you to have a thought race through your mind. The simple fact is that we people cannot not think."

But there's more. Humans are not only thrown to think, but, unlike other beings, they're also thrown to think abstractly. They naturally form concepts. They reason and judge. They make meaning of their experiences, remember events from the past, and imagine the future.

Consider, for example, an incident from just last night. I came home from work and settled into my easy chair. My black lab Jake trotted over and sat between my legs, his face tilted upward, his eyes fixed on mine. He did not bark or whimper, the only sound was his tail swishing the floor as I stroked his head.

I held his gaze, thinking how stupid it was for me to engage in a staring contest with a dog. Then, for fun, I said to him, "Hey, Jake, how about if I tell you a little joke?"

Jake did not react. He continued to sit and stare, though his tail wagging escalated at the sound of my voice.

"So," I said, "did you hear the one about the depressed dyslexic? No? Well, he threw himself *behind* the bus."

Jake registered no expression at all. He did not smile, chuckle, or roll his eyes. All he did was continue to wag his tail and look at me with his blank, uncomprehending eyes. Point made.

2. The Contextual Nature of Human Cognition

To unpack the contextual nature of the ABCs of REBT, let me first share with you the initial part of my first psychotherapy session with Kathy, one of my current patients. She walked into my office on a sweltering July afternoon that the air conditioner barely kept at bay. Dressed in a blue skirt and blouse, her streaked blonde hair cut short and swept back, she displayed the professional appearance of the corporate manager that she was. But her downcast eyes and slumped shoulders betrayed a sense of gloom, perhaps defeat, as she handed me her intake papers. In the section titled, "Major Problems," she wrote: "Very depressed—help!"

I got right down to business by asking Kathy about what she was depressed.

With eyes lowered, she took in a deep breath and, in almost a whisper, said, "I've failed at so many things, but mostly with my children."

She paused and sighed. Then, with tear-filled eyes, she told me about her daughter, who was pregnant, alcoholic, and unemployed, and about her youngest, a son, who was also seriously depressed because of a recent divorce. "Look at what's happened to them. I've done so many things wrong in my life, so many things."

"Will you share what you think you've done that was so wrong?"

"Like raising them so strict. Like going overboard with all that hellfire and brimstone religious stuff. Like not protecting them from their abusive father. I did nothing right. Everything I did led them to this point."

Kathy pulled two tissues of Kleenex from the box on the end table next to her and dabbed at the corners of her eyes. She sat limp and sighed.

"But, look, Kathy," I said, making sure to maintain eye contact, "you're not depressed because of the mistakes you've made. You're depressed because of what you're telling yourself about your mistakes. What is it?"

"That's easy. As their mother, I owed them so much more."

"So, what I hear you telling yourself is two things. One, 'I didn't parent them as well as I wanted to.' Two, 'I should have done better and not made the mistakes I did. Therefore I'm a terrible mother.' Right?"

Her eyes darted to mine, then back to her hands clasped on her lap. "I've never felt worth anything. How could I, with my mother constantly belittling me, telling me I was a mistake child, saying over and over she wished I were dead. If this doesn't prove that she was right, I don't know what does."

"So your depression goes beyond damning yourself for your parenting. You're also damning yourself for other things—for failing to get your mother to love you, for marrying your husband, for staying with him, and for God knows what else. And you've been doing this to yourself for many years by now. Right?"

"Yes."

"That kind of thinking would make anyone depressed, Kathy."

In a tragic tone, she said, "But it's true, I am a failure."

"Well," I said, raising my voice an octave or two to interrupt her mental path, "that self-damning thinking is what we've got to knock out of your head—that you shouldn't have made the mistakes you've made, that you're a bad mother, and, furthermore, that you're a bad person. I'm here to help you do that. Once we do, you'll find yourself no longer depressed."

"Good luck with that," she said, her eyes still cast to her lap. "I've never felt worthy. Never. I don't even know what that would feel like."

Through my work with patients like Kathy, I came to see that human cognition can be separated into three categories, from the most concrete and specific to the more general and philosophic (see Figure 1.1). I assume three propositions: (1) the more general and philosophic the cognition, the more likely the cognition is to be unarticulated, that is, beyond conscious awareness; (2) the more general and philosophic the cognition, the more pervasively the cognition is likely to influence a person's life across situations; (3) the more general and philosophic the

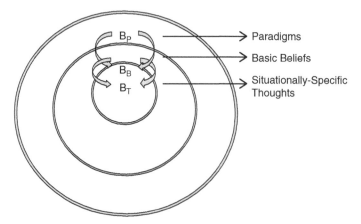

Figure 1.1 Human cognition contextualized

cognition, the more likely it is to influence a person's belief systems and thought patterns.

Contextualized from the inside-out, they are:

- Situationally specific thoughts or self-talks about events a person experiences in day-to-day life (B_T);
- general beliefs a person holds about oneself, other people, or the world across all situations (B_B);[4]
- paradigms, that is, a person's core constructs that underlie and spawn one's beliefs and situationally specific thinking (B_P).

Back to Kathy. Notice, first, the situationally specific thoughts (at B_T) that she believed to be true about herself: (1) I failed with my children; (2) I shouldn't have made the mistakes I did with them; (3) I'm, therefore, a failure as a mother and a person.

But it was no accident that Kathy entertained these self-damning thoughts in response to her children's turmoil. Why? Because of the indoctrination throughout her childhood by her mother about her worthlessness, she had adopted an overarching belief about herself (at B_B) that molded how she thought across all situations: I am a failure, virtually worthless as a human being. With this belief lodged in her brain, Kathy had little choice but to condemn herself as a horrible mother and person (at B_T) for what she believed to be her parenting mistakes.

But this doesn't tell the whole story. Kathy's specific thoughts (B_T) and her more general beliefs (B_B) were themselves both contextualized within and molded by her paradigms (B_P).[5] Paradigms are not the content of what one believes, nor are they the specific thoughts that race through a person's mind on a moment-to-moment basis. Rather, they are the most general principles, models, or worldviews, often unrecognized and unarticulated, that guide and set the context of all of one's perceptions, thoughts, and beliefs, as well as, ultimately, how one feels and acts in life.

Kathy revealed in our conversation that she endorsed two paradigms (B_P) from which what she believed (B_B) derived and which inevitably spawned what she thought across situations (B_T). One we call Self-Rating. In this paradigm, she held that it is appropriate and justifiable to rate, judge, or esteem herself in her entirety as either all good or all bad. Note that this paradigm set the stage for esteeming herself at B_B as worthless and thinking of herself at B_T as a failure for failing as a parent. The second paradigm we call Perfectionistic Demanding in which she endorsed the concept that there is an absolute universal command or demand, an expectation if you will, that she must always do and be perfect in whatever she does.

So, these two paradigms set the context for her belief about herself to be a worthless failure, which in turn prompted her to think in the specific self-damning ways that caused her depression when she faced perceived parental failure. And all this nonsense—at B_T, B_B, and B_P—I would have to help Kathy remove and replace in order for her to have a thorough, elegant cure of her depression.

3. A Cognitive Creation of Reality

The Contextual ABC Model makes a distinction between the circumstances *in* one's life and the experiences one has *of* the circumstances in one's life (see Figure 1.2). While there is indeed a real world of circumstances (matter and events) that does exist "out there" (the A), this real world differs from the one in which we relate and respond. What we humans deal with are the circumstances colored and molded by our selective attention, perceptual interpretations, and evaluative beliefs (the A'). In actuality, nothing exists for us without this interpretative/evaluating mental processing. The rub is that people are usually unaware of this process and assume that what they "see" accurately represents the truth about what exists "in the world."

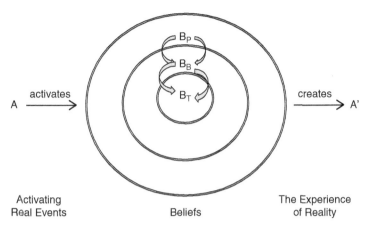

Figure 1.2 The cognitive creation of reality

This is exactly what Kathy did to create her own reality (A'). The truth is that she behaved properly toward her children a great deal of the time. Nevertheless, she filtered the reality of this (the A) through her beliefs about herself as a worthless failure to create the reality she experienced of herself as a mother (A'). She then selectively focused exclusively on her mothering mistakes and thereby generalized from the few mistakes she did make to cast all of her mothering behaviors in that light. Consequently, her perceptual reality (at A') amounted to: "I did nothing right. Everything I did led them to this point."

Thus, in the Contextual ABC Model, people like Kathy often start themselves down the path to emotional disturbance by creating a distorted, negative picture of their reality, their A'. In REBT, then, it is important to help people understand and change the ways by which at B they create their reality of Events (A'), as well as to help them change the ways they also create their emotional and behavioral reactions (at C) to their self-created reality.

4. The Cognitive Creation of Consequences

It is axiomatic to the ABCs of REBT that the beliefs people impose on their perceived reality (A') causes how they react

18   THE NATURE OF BEING HUMAN

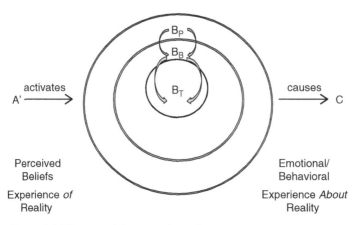

Figure 1.3 The cognitive creation of consequences

emotionally and behaviorally (see Figure 1.3). Yet, while people can have any number of thoughts about their experienced Activating Event, these thoughts are rarely random or accidental. To the contrary, the thinking people do at B_T is strongly molded by their higher beliefs (B_B) and by their bedrock paradigms (B_P).

Then, following REBT, the interaction of A' and the contextualized Bs (B_T, B_B, B_P) strongly influences the person's emotional and behavioral reactions. In other words, the thinking (B_T) that people do mediates between A' and C and therefore can be said to "cause" or "create" C. When thinking is done at B_T in the context of the belief in Perfectionistic Demanding and/or Self-Rating, as in Kathy's case, C usually consists of emotional disturbance (e.g., severe feelings of depression, anxiety, guilt, and/or anger).

5. The Cognitive-Philosophic Cure

Over the years I've worked with patients who've experienced just about every imaginable reaction to their emotional problems. A few take them in stride, much like they would if they suffered from the common cold. Others feel scared, fearing that they're doomed to a life of emotional misery. Others feel ashamed, embarrassed, even humiliated, as if their troubles are tattooed on them forever as a sign of terminal weakness or some form of moral depravity. Still others react with depression, despondent that they are forced to deal with their emotional burdens on top of life's other problems.

To all these people I offer reassurance. I tell them they're not hopeless, depraved, or weak, for, after all, they do not suffer from some mysterious, exotic, or terminal illness, but, thank God, only the effects of having learned and endorsed irrational paradigms, beliefs, and thought patterns that cause their symptomology. These they've learned and, therefore, they can unlearn. I reassure them that they can and will get better, provided they commit to working hard with me.

This I did with Kathy. I had already explained to her the ABCs of her depression, showed her the connection between her thinking at B and her misery at C, and alluded to the fact that her thoughts about her parenting were quite contextualized in deeply endorsed beliefs and paradigms. I emphasized that our therapeutic purpose was to seek the truth about herself, whatever that might be, using the philosopher's tools of reason and logic and the scientist's tool of empirical data.

Then I said to her, "Look, Kathy, we know beyond a shadow of a doubt that your self-damning causes your depression: the belief that you shouldn't have made the mistakes you did with your kids, and that you're a terrible person for having done so. Using reason and logic, is that belief true or valid?"

Without a second's hesitation, she said, "Of course I shouldn't have."

I noticed the force behind her words, the adamant cast to her eyes. But I persisted. "So, Kathy, you think you should have been the perfect mom and shouldn't have made the mistakes you did. Is that a reasonable expectation for you or any other mother?"

"Well, I can make some mistakes, but not those."

"So your logic tells you that it's reasonable for you to expect to make at least some mistakes in your parenting. Yes?"

"Yeeesss," she said, drawing the word out, a message I interpreted to communicate wariness.

"Now, remember, Kathy, all we're after here is the truth, whatever that may be, not some good-sounding crap to make you feel better. So let's bore in a bit to see if we can find some truth here. Why is it logical to expect to make mistakes in your role as a mother?"

"Because I'm human," she said in a tone that sounded more like a question than a statement, as if that answer were too simple to be true.

"That's right," I said, careful to keep my voice calm and steady. "But when you say, 'I'm human,' what does that mean?"

I focused intently on Kathy, looking for signs of resistance. I saw her tilt her head, purse her lips, and peer into the distance in a way that communicated she was chewing over the question.

"Humans all make mistakes," she finally said.

"That's right," I said, putting force behind my words, "all humans are fallible and make mistakes. You too, Kathy. You're not a special case. You too make mistakes, because you're also a fallible human being, an error-prone, talented mistake-maker, like all the rest of us. As such, you must error, must make mistakes, and must have faults, in every single role you play in life, including that of motherhood. Right?"

She nodded.

"Furthermore, you must have the faults you do and make the mistakes you make, when and where you make them, not just the ones you find desirable or convenient. Those are the truths about human nature, aren't they?"

"They are," she said.

I had brought Kathy to a critical point where she might, just might, entertain a better way to think about herself.

Steady, be careful, I told myself, then pressed on.

"Good. Now let's push forward just a step or two more before we reschedule. Look, both of these statements can't be true: one, being human and fallible, 'I must have faults and must make mistakes as a parent;' or, two, 'I don't care that I'm human and fallible, I still shouldn't and I'll be damned for it.' Now, use your reason, not your automatic habit of thought, and tell me which of these two statements are true?"

She expelled a long sigh, then said, "Obviously the former, but ..."

"No buts, Kathy," I said, interrupting. "We're into pure reason and logic here, in the service of finding the truth, not into you mindlessly re-propagandizing yourself with your pre-existing thoughts and beliefs. So, as a fallible human being, is it reasonable or logical for you or any mother to bring up children error-free, without any fault? Now, think about it logically. What's the answer?"

"No, it's not reasonable," she said, "but it still wasn't good what I did, was it?"

"Of course not, you made mistakes," I said, leaning forward. "But, what if you gave up that perfectionistic, self-damning belief, 'I shouldn't have made the mistakes I did, damn me,' and replaced it with, 'I'm sorry that I made those mistakes, but I'm a fallible human, so what can I learn from them to do better going forward?' You'd feel regretful and sorrowful, but not guilty and depressed. Then you'd have the best of both worlds; you'd be rid of your depression and still motivated to be good at moming. Not a bad deal, is it?"

"Then what?" she said.

"Then you love the living daylights out of your kids going forward."

"This is going to take some time," she said.

"I know it will," I said, smiling, "but not as much as you might think, that is, if you commit to truth-telling rather than mindlessly regurgitating the same old ideas over and over like you've been doing. Okay?"

"Okay," she said.

I leaned forward and fixed my eyes on hers. "Kathy, I'll put everything I have into helping you change the way you think about yourself, both with regard to your kids and in more general terms, so you can get rid of that damn depression once and for all. Will you make the same commitment to me?"

"I will," she said, raising her right hand oath-like.

"Great," I said, "let's kick ass."

Kathy smiled for the first time since she walked into my office. So did I.

That concluded Kathy's first psychotherapy session. Notice how deeply I got to know her through this initial conversation. I didn't know her social or academic history, much of the details of her childhood, her hobbies, her sexual preferences. But I got to know her at the very center of who she was as a human being—her most cherished desires and values, her core paradigms and beliefs about herself, her deepest vulnerabilities. What a privilege it was to be able to connect with a human being at such an intimate level. What a responsibility it carried.

Reflection

It is now May, 2017, almost thirty-seven years since I resigned my tenured Associate Professor position at the University of Virginia to embark on a career as a practicing clinical psychologist. These years have been rich and rewarding, ones that have afforded me the opportunity to fulfill my dream of a career practicing psychotherapy and, along the way, learn so very much.

Foremost in what I've learned is that, to be effective, a psychotherapist must be grounded in a sound conceptualization of the nature of being human. With such a conceptualization, the therapist can go right to the core cause of a patient's problems, select the most efficacious treatment strategies, and keep oneself and the patient focused on doing what's necessary to bring about lasting change. Without such a conceptualization, the therapist will be little more than a technician, trying one strategy after another, hoping one will bring about symptom relief.

Through my experience, I am convinced that the ABCs of REBT get right to the heart of being human. It communicates that the human mind—with its capacity to perceive, think, hold beliefs and paradigms—defines who we are and causes us to show up in life as we do emotionally, behaviorally, even physiologically. Emotional disturbance comes about when a person comes to endorse and acts on beliefs that are unrealistic and irrational, and cure takes place when a person replaces these with more realistic, rational ones.

Someone once complained to Albert Ellis that his ABC model of human nature was much too simple. He responded: "Yes, but simple does not mean it's not true. The wheel is simple, but it took humanity thousands of years to discover it. Once it did, it revolutionized the world."

Everything I do in my clinical office flows from my conviction that the human mind is the core of what it means to be human—all the strategies and techniques I employ. Moreover, everything I've learned throughout the years, things maybe not in the textbooks, I have learned through the framework of REBT's ABCs. And, everything I teach my patients starts with the premise: you think yourself into disturbance, and you have to think yourself out of it.

If I may share a desire with you, it's that you adopt the ABCs as your own truth about human nature and use it in your practice as a therapist or on yourself as a person in your own right. But, if you choose not to, I implore you to do whatever it takes to define for yourself your own belief as to what is the nature of being human. After all, this is the nexus around which all therapeutic decisions need to be made.

Notes

1 Originally called Rational Emotive Therapy (RET), Albert Ellis changed its name to Rational Emotive Behavior Therapy (REBT) in 1995. I will use the term Rational Emotive Behavior Therapy throughout the remainder of this book regardless of what it was called at the time of the events I describe.
2 I cannot tell from my notes whether the demonstration with Joyce took place that afternoon at the APA convention or whether I watched it on another occasion live or via videotape. Nevertheless, from many observations of Albert Ellis doing REBT, I can attest to the fact that this demonstration accurately represents the REBT process as practiced and taught by him.
3 See Grieger, R. M. (1985). From a Linear to a Contextual Model of the ABC's of RET. *Journal of Rational Emotive Therapy*, Vol. 3, No. 2, pp. 75–99.
4 These in turn are subdivided into Perceptual Beliefs (habitual inferences and interpretations made from raw sensory data) and Evaluative Beliefs (beliefs that impose values or judgment upon the perceived events).
5 REBT identified four irrational paradigms that individually or collectively spawned almost all emotional disturbance. Each can be seen as a dichotomy between two poles; at any given moment a person stands at one pole or the other, but rarely, if ever, with a foot at both. (1) *Perfectionistic Demanding*, in which one holds that there is an absolute, universal imperative that commands oneself, other people, and life situations to be perfect, as opposed to *Practical Preferring*, in which one holds that, no matter how preferable it may be to do well and have life be benevolent, it is only desirable, not necessary; (2) *Catastrophizing*, in which one habitually rates hassles and hardships as horrors, as opposed to *Perspective*, in which one rates the degree of any frustration only as bad as it realistically is; (3) *Low Frustration Tolerance*, in which one views difficulty or pain as unbearable or unstandable, as opposed to *High Frustration Tolerance*, in which one views setbacks and difficulties as undesirable but endurable; and (4) *Self-Rating*, whereby one holds it is possible, appropriate, and justifiable to totally rate, judge, or esteem a person in one's entirety as either all good or all bad, as opposed to *Self-Acceptance*, in which one holds that, while it is appropriate and even beneficial to rate one's performances and traits, people are too complex and multifaceted to ever be totally rated or evaluated in their entirety as all good or all bad.

2

THE POWER OF PASSIONATE PURPOSE

The fuel that stimulates sustained high energy, enthusiasm, and satisfaction

> *All men dream: but not equally.*
> *Those who dream by night*
> *in the dusty recesses of their mind*
> *wake in the day to find that it was vanity;*
> *but the dreamers of the day are dangerous men,*
> *for they may act on their dreams with open eyes,*
> *to make it possible.*
> – *T. E. Lawrence*, Lawrence of Arabia

This moving and empowering quote from T. E. Lawrence's 1926 memoir, *Seven Pillars of Wisdom* (Lawrence, 1926) always reminds me of how important it is for a person to have a passionate purpose in life. Mine began to take shape on one of those sticky August evenings in Charlottesville that makes you long for autumn. I stood outside the Omni Hotel at the west end of the Downtown Mall where I had just delivered an after-dinner address to the Rotary Club. Though dusk had settled in, the mall still bustled with life. Street vendors stood behind tables hawking their wares. Couples strolled and window-shopped. The faint sound of a busker strumming his guitar floated through the air.

Just as I took off my jacket and loosened my tie, a well-dressed man in a dark blue business suit walked up to me, extended his hand, and said, "That was a powerful talk."

"Glad you liked it," I said. "At least it took us out of this heat."

Chuckling, he said, "You know, you should go national with that."

Little did this gentleman know that I had considered the same thing. I had maintained for years a vibrant clinical practice and developed a robust organizational consulting business. Students seemed to appreciate my seminars.

Nevertheless, I felt frustrated. Instead of laboring one-on-one in my clinical office or in groups of fifteen in business conference rooms, I wanted to fill stadiums, go platinum with my personal empowerment CDs, host nationwide closed-circuit video conferences. What I wanted was to swim in a big pond, be a Tony Robbins, a Dr. Phil, a Stephen Covey.

I walked east on the mall toward the parking garage. I passed trendy restaurants serving customers sitting outdoors under umbrellas, the Paramount Theater where a line snaked in front of storefronts to get in to see Emmylou Harris, an ice cream parlor where people savored scoops of their favorite flavor. Lost in thought, I barely noticed. By the time I reached my car, I knew I had to do something about my situation.

Bright and early the next morning, I arranged monthly telephone sessions with a personal coach named Margaret. She lived in Colorado. To this day, I have no idea what she looks like, nor do I know anything about the details of her life. I only know her by her voice—deep, bordering on husky, clear and precise, straight arrow. But, because of one conversation we had on the night of September 20, she has become one of the most significant people in my life.

It started with what sounded like an innocuous question. "So, let me ask, what's unique about you?"

I thought for a moment, then answered honestly, "Nothing, really. I have talents, but none unique. Other people have the same ones I do."

"There you have it," she said, her voice deeper, her pace measured, emphasizing each word almost as a separate thought.

"What?"

"What you just said is so limiting. You have no chance of reaching your goals until you figure out what differentiates you from the thousands of others out there who have your same aspirations."

I sat silent, not knowing what to say.

Finally she broke the silence. "Now, listen carefully. I want you to interview six people who know you intimately. Ask them: 'What do I bring to the table that is unique about me? What distinguishes me from all the others?' Will you do that?"

The very next evening I sat in my living room and called each of the six people I identified. I told them the reason behind my call and made my request, emphasizing that I wanted them to be brutally honest, even if they had negative feedback.

The first five promised their answers within a week. The sixth, Jim, whose company I had consulted with for the past two years, didn't hesitate. He simply said, "Get paper and pencil and I'll tell you exactly what's unique about you."

"Now?"

"Yeah, now. Get the paper and pencil."

I did and settled back in my recliner, my notepad on my lap, my pencil poised. "Go," I said.

"Okay, here goes. What's unique about you is that you take a solid stand to make people's lives perfect, as they want it. That's what you do. It runs through everything. It's so inspiring that it's unusual for somebody to not participate with you."

I sat amazed, stunned actually, for the second he said it, I realized that's exactly what I try to do with every one of my patients, my organizational clients, my students.

I said nothing. Neither did Jim. Finally I rallied. "Damn, Jim, you nailed it, but I had never consciously put that into words until you said it to me."

"Well, it's true. I've seen you in action. You simply don't veer from that."

Wired, I couldn't sit still or make small talk. Nothing else needed to be said. I said my goodbyes, walked from the living room into the kitchen, opened and closed the refrigerator door without retrieving anything, then returned empty-handed to my recliner. I rolled around in my mind what Jim had said as if it were a piece of caramel candy that I wanted to savor without swallowing.

Sometimes a truth comes in layers, one layer building on top of the one before, until the whole of it is so obvious that it seems like it had always been there. That evening the rest of truth came to me instantly, clear and whole.

I understood that what Jim said was true: I try to help every person I work with make their lives perfect, as they want it. But, that was only half of it. I also understood that all that really mattered was that I act on my purpose. I didn't need to go national, become famous, make millions of dollars annually. All that—the fame, money, glamour—were mere trappings. I understood that the only thing that I needed to change was my perspective, not my clinical practice, organizational consulting, or teaching. All I needed to do was to keep on doing what I already did, but with that purpose consciously held forefront in my mind.

I settled back in my recliner. My wife Patti walked in and settled on the couch next to my recliner. My face must have betrayed something, for she asked, "Are you okay?"

"Better than okay," I said, and told her about my revelation.

"That's awesome, Honey. I've been saying all along that you make an incredible difference in people's lives."

"I try," I said, grinning, "but it's your job to say things like that, so I just ignore it."

"Oh, right," she said, grinning back.

Fast forward to today. Each morning before I go to the office, I take a minute or so to reconnect to my passionate purpose for doing the work I do—that is, to do my best to make people's lives perfect, as they want it. When I am aligned with it, magic happens. I care deeply about the person I'm with. Time seems to both slow down and pass bullet-fast. I feel alive, empowered. My focus is sharp. I persist through frustration, resistance, resentment, filled with enthusiasm and wonder. My satisfaction and happiness escalate.

I share this personal story for two reasons. One is to illustrate the profound benefits of passionate purpose to both the professional performance and personal fulfillment of the psychotherapist. It can stimulate, empower, give satisfaction.

A second reason is to suggest that developing a passionate purpose can be of tremendous value for many patients. After all, psychotherapy can be more than about just alleviating unhappiness. Once anxiety, depression, guilt, and/or anger are conquered, it can then aid and abet fulfillment, satisfaction, and happiness as well.

Take, for example, my patient, Michael, a middle-aged minister who took a leave-of-absence from his parish duties because of a severe depression disorder. He embraced REBT's ABCs, worked hard at his therapy, and gradually erased the self-damning beliefs that drove his depression. Though feeling much better emotionally, he still found it difficult to get out of bed before noon, attend to household chores, and resume his ministerial duties. Try as I might, I couldn't budge him.

Just this morning, he had a breakthrough. It started when I asked him, "Michael, you're thinking so much more rationally than when we first met, feeling so much better. Now, put on your thinking cap and answer this question: What's holding you back from once again embracing life? Is it a fear of failure, perhaps a fear of sliding back into depression?"

He thought for a moment, his chin cupped in his hand, gazing over my shoulder, then said, "No, I don't think so."

"Then what about feeling guilty and ashamed for being imperfect and getting yourself depressed?"

"No, not really," he said, this time without hesitation. "I just think, 'Why bother to get up. There's nothing to do today.'"

"Oh, I get it," I said, smiling. "It's not really that you literally have nothing to do, but that you don't see meaning in what is in your life. With no purpose behind it, why bother. What do you think? Did I get it right?"

"By Golly, you did," he said, then again stared over my shoulder. After a few seconds, he remade eye contact and asked, "So, what do I do about that?"

"Well, we've got to get you back in touch with your purpose in becoming a minister to begin with. Do you remember what that was?"

Without pausing, he said, "I do—to spread the love of God."

"How'd you do that?"

"Through my sermons. Performing marriages. Visiting the sick in the hospital. Counseling with people who've lost their faith, those with troubled marriages, those grieving for a loved one. With everything."

As I listened, I noticed that Michael had scooted to the front of his seat. His eyes brightened and he became more animated.

"That's great, Michael," I said. "The overarching 'why' of your life is to spread the love of God through your ministry. It got you out of bed each morning with a zip in your step. Yes?"

"For sure."

"So, let me ask you this question: did that purpose spread out to the other parts of your life as well—perhaps with your wife and kids, your friends, whatever?"

A slight smile crossed his face, followed by a drawn-out "Uuh." Then he said, "You know, I never thought about it, but I guess I did act that out in the rest of my life, without realizing it. Wow!"

"Wow is right," I said, giving him the thumbs up signal. "Does spreading the love of God still resonate with you?"

"Absolutely."

"Okay then," I said, "before we part today, I want two commitments from you, if you're willing. First, will you commit to working hard to infuse this purpose back into your life?"

"Yes, I will."

"Hand to God?" I said, raising my hand oath-like and smiling.

He mimicked me, smiling back, and repeated, "I will."

"Great, Michael. Now, second, I make it a rule of thumb, as you know, to never leave a therapy session without the patient committing to translate into action what was discussed. So, let's identify three actions you will commit to do every day between now and our next session. They can be big, medium, or small, but with this caveat—you have to do them with the express purpose of spreading the love of God. Will you?"

Michael agreed. He committed to take his dog for a walk each morning, do at least one ministerial chore each day, and spend at least one hour of quality time with his wife each afternoon or evening.

When we parted, he shook my hand and then pulled me into a bearhug. While I did not do classic REBT this day with Michael, as that work had already been done, he and I did focus on a powerful belief outside the REBT mainstream—that is, Michael's belief about the purpose of his life. I am convinced that, with that belief restored to the forefront of his mind, along with his newfound self-acceptance belief, he will find it not only easy, but compelling, to get out of bed and skip back into his life.

Reflection

Consider that there are three levels at which one can live. On the first level, one does one's best to keep busy, engage in entertaining activities, create as much enjoyment as possible. While there is nothing intrinsically wrong with this, there are no overarching goals, no passionate purpose to life. Consequently, there is little opportunity for pride, fulfillment, or happiness.

Level two is when one centers life around accomplishing valued goals. Typical ones include developing a successful career, creating a happy marriage and family, building financial security. The possibility for pleasure and satisfaction is certainly greater at this level than the first, for what one does is oriented around activities that have deep personal meaning.

But it is when one lives at level three that passion can be aroused, excitement ignited, joy and fulfillment attained. To live at this level, one must first figure out the burning "why"—the passionate purpose—of one's life, and then express it throughout the fabric of one's life.

Before providing a step-by-step process to do just that, I want to first offer you three perspectives on passionate purpose:

1. It is about creating, not discovering. In discovering, you find the life's purpose that is predetermined for you. The problem with this approach is that you have to take it on faith that you do indeed have a predetermined purpose, a dubious assumption at best. Creating is about determining for yourself what your life's purpose is. It is about what holds meaning for you, what excites and drives you.
2. Distinguish between goals and purpose. Goals refer to specific outcomes you wish to accomplish with certain people and/or certain outcomes. For example, my goal with Michael is to get him active in his family, social, and ministerial life. This goal, though, is in the service of my passionate purpose, to help him make his life perfect, as he personally wants.
3. Keep an eye on life as a whole, not just on one or two specific roles you play in life. I, for example, am one and the same person across all situations, my role as a psychotherapist being just one of several. Imagine the passion and power I can bring across the spectrum of my life by always acting to help people make their lives perfect, as they want it—including myself.

Now I share with you a three-step process to create passionate purpose.[1] I give credit to Steve Covey (1989) for its structure. I encourage you, the psychotherapist, to first work your way through this process for your own benefit, and then use it with your patients as they may communicate a need for it.

Step One: Reflect on Your Purpose

With paper and pencil, thoughtfully reflect on the following five questions. These provide a basis for getting in touch with your deepest, most cherished values, pleasures, and desires. They can spawn the material for creating your life's purpose. For each, I will cite its source and explain how it is significant to developing your purpose, as well as illustrate it from my own experience.

1. What am I doing when I am in the flow?

"Flow" is a term coined by the eminent psychiatrist Mihaly Csikszentmihalyi in his seminal book, *Flow* (1991). It refers to a state in which you are so focused that everything else but what you are doing disappears. Time seems to stand still. You are totally absorbed. What you are doing seems effortless and rewarding. When in the flow, you are most likely engaged in an activity that has deep personal significance to you.

I can identify three activities in my life in which I experienced flow. When I was younger, I played high school and college basketball, playing on two NCAA Championship teams. I remember being so absorbed playing the game that the spectators, coaches, and, to some extent, other players often seemed to disappear. I was aware of what was going on around me, of course, but my awareness was limited to just playing basketball. The court, the basketball, and even the other players became pawns for my creative expression.

In my current life, I frequently experience flow when doing psychotherapy. I am absorbed in the inner world of my patients, lose track of time, and feel a deep connection with them. Another flow experience is when I interact with workshop participants about some cogent issue of character or personality that I believe can be life transforming. In these activities, I frequently become so absorbed that I wish the encounter would never end.

Now is an opportunity for you to reflect on your own life experiences and identify times when you too are in the flow. Describe below three of these. What were you doing? What were you feeling? Most importantly, what meaning can you draw from what you were doing?

1.

2.

3.

2. What is unique about me?

I've already related in detail the story about my professional frustrations and the solution I experienced through my work with Margaret, my personal coach. I now urge you to uncover your uniqueness. As I did, I suggest you enlist the observations and insights of trusted friends or colleagues. Take sufficient time to identify six people, contact them, and get their feedback as to what is unique about you. Write what they say below:

Person 1 –

Person 2 –

Person 3 –

Person 4 –

Person 5 –

Person 6 –

3. About what am I enthusiastic?

Many people waste their time trying to fire themselves up. They invent all kinds of strategies to excite themselves into action. While this may work for a brief period, enthusiasm cannot be sustained through gimmickry.

The quest now before you is to uncover what it is that excites your enthusiasm. For example, I am enthusiastic about helping my clinical patients and my business consultees defeat the problems they face and evolve into all they can be. I am also enthusiastic about helping my sons develop strength of character. And I am enthusiastic about helping and supporting my wife in her pursuit of happiness in life.

As you address this question, be careful to note that you may not be enthusiastic about some particular activity, but only about the reason for doing it. I distinctly remember a housewife telling me she enthusiastically went about the onerous chore of cleaning her bathrooms. Seeing the incredulous look on my face, she explained that she saw this chore as an expression of taking loving care of her family.

Now reflect on your enthusiasms. What lights your fire? What turns you on? What do you deeply care about? The answers to these questions, along with what about them excites you, will help you create your life's passionate purpose.

> 4. What could I do in life that would provide
> the most value, make the biggest contribution,
> and have the most positive impact?

In helping people proactively take charge of their lives, Stephen Covey poses two profound questions:

1. "What is one thing that, if you did it consistently and excellently, would make a profoundly positive difference in your personal life?"
2. "What is one thing that, if you did it consistently and excellently, would make a profoundly positive difference in your professional life?"

My experience is that it takes people little time or effort to answer these questions. The next and perhaps more important question to ask is, "If you know these would make such a difference, why would you want to do them?"

Both the "what" and the "why not" questions are empowering. The "what" questions alert you to what exactly you need to do to produce great results. The "why not" question communicates that it is your responsibility to transcend the "reasons" for not doing what's necessary to make these results a reality.

Knowing the answers to these questions can also help you create your passionate purpose. Now, please reflect on this question: what could you do that would have the most value, make the most positive impact, and make the biggest contribution in both your personal and professional life? To add meat to this question, make sure you note who would benefit and how—You? Your loved ones? Your friends and colleagues? Your clientele? Society at large?

In my personal life:

In my professional life:

5. What kind of person would I like to be?

To help you with this question, think of one or two people whom you most admire and have made a big impact on your life. What qualities do they possess?

When I asked myself this question, I was able to identify six people. They were my mother and father; my English Literature teacher in college, Dr. Paul Grabel; my college basketball coach, Arad McCutchan; my psychology mentor, Dr. Albert Ellis; and my cousin, Bill Stocker. Each of these cherished individuals possessed qualities that I have attempted to integrate into my character. And they have helped give meaning to my life.

I am sure you can easily identify at least two significant people of your own. Do so now, along with their notable qualities. This too can contribute to you creating your purpose.

The Persons	Their Notable Qualities
1.	
2.	

Step Two: Create Your Purpose

Now that you are armed with all this introspective information, your second step in this workshop is to create your life's purpose. One of the mistakes people often make is to rush this step. Instead, take your time and reflect on your answers to the five questions posed above. You might want to carry the answers with you for a week or so and make additions or corrections as you go along. You might also want to make notes about themes or phrases you want included in your purpose before creating it.

Your purpose can be written in any format that communicates to you. It can be a single phrase, a poem, a sentence, a brief paragraph, or even a song or a picture. The point is that your purpose must speak to you without concern for what others may think. It is meant to reflect your passion and spark your drive and fulfillment.

By the way of example, I offer Mike Krzyzewski, the Duke University basketball coach, holder of three NCAA championship trophies, two Olympic gold medals, and more wins than anyone else in NCAA history. He said, "I am not a basketball coach. I am a leader who coaches basketball. I have three goals with all my players—to make them a good student, a good citizen, and a good person."

Another example is the Purpose Statement of Mahatma Gandhi (Johnson, 2006) who liberated India from the rule of Great Britain by acting according to his non-violent passionate philosophy:

"Let the first act of every morning be to make the following resolve for the day:

I shall not fear anyone on earth.
I shall only fear God.
I shall not bear ill toward anyone.
I shall not submit to injustice from anyone.

*I shall conquer untruth by truth.
And, in resisting untruth, I shall put up
with all suffering."*

Lastly, I remind you of my own example discovered through my coaching experience with Margaret. It is: to make people's lives perfect, as they want it.

Now it is time to create your Purpose. Remember to review the answers to your reflection questions and follow the guidelines above. Once you have penned a first draft, carry it with you. Reflect on it. Make notes about changes you might want. After a week or two, compose your final version.

My Purpose

(First draft)

Step Three: Live Your Purpose

Now you have your life's purpose in hand. While it hopefully inspires you, it is most likely too general to be of much practical use. To take it to the level of useful action, you need to plan exactly how you will express it throughout the fabric of your life.

Stephen Covey (1989) wisely suggests that the major roles we play in life can serve as vehicles through which to live out our purpose. I, for example, took my purpose and articulated how I would express it through the following five roles:

- Myself,
- My wife and sons,
- My extended family and friends,
- My clinical and consulting practices,
- My teaching.

The question I asked myself was: "how can I help the person or people in each of these roles make their lives perfect, as they want it?" In asking this question, I was surprised that the answers stimulated me to create additional work activities that excited me even further and gave me additional opportunities to express my purpose. I might add that writing this book is one important way I discovered to live my purpose through my work.

So, the next step in your workshop is to clearly articulate ways to express your purpose through each major role you play in your life. You can borrow my categories or articulate your own. By connecting what you do to this purpose, how can your days not be filled with passion, drive, and satisfaction? How can you not be driven to act out your purpose? How can you not create the extraordinary results you define as significant?

My Roles　　　How Can I Express My Purpose

1.

2.

3.

A final point. There is nothing magical to it. Creating and making use of passionate purpose is a process. If Michael and I can create and live by our passionate purposes, fully reaping the benefits, so can you—and your patients. All it takes is determination, dedication, and hard work.

Note

1 This workshop is adopted from chapter 3, The Power of Passionate Purpose, of my book, *Developing Unrelenting Drive, Dedication, and Determination. A Cognitive Behavior Workbook*, published by Routledge in 2017.

References

Covey, S. A. (1989). *The 7 Habits of Highly Effective People.* New York: Simon & Schuster.

Csikszentmihalyi, M. (1991). *Flow.* New York: Basic Books.

Johnson, R. L. (2006). *Gandhi's Experiments with Truth: Essential Writing by and About Gandhi.* Washington, D.C.: Rowman and Littlefield.

Lawrence, T. E. (1926). *Seven Pillars of Wisdom.* New York: Doubleday & Company, Inc.

3

FEARLESSNESS

The courage to do what is needed

*They are surely to be esteemed
the bravest spirits who,
having the clearest sense of both
the pains and pleasures of life,
do not on the account
shrink from danger.*
— Thucydides

The practice of psychotherapy brings with it the same personal challenges one finds in all aspects of life: confusion and self-doubt, the possibility of making mistakes, incurring disapproval, out and out failure, even doing damage to a patient despite the best of intentions. With these possibilities always in play, it behooves the psychotherapist to be fearless, to have the courage to make the tough calls, risk mistakes, and to accept the fact that not every patient will be satisfied.

Sabrina presented me with many of these challenges. I first met her on a bitter December evening a few days before Christmas. A mixture of freezing rain and icy snow pelted the window. I felt weary, having already spent a full day in intense conversation with nine patients who were themselves steeped in their own emotional quagmires.

In she walked, slow and expressionless, eyes downcast and shoulders slumped. I noted her light brown skin, close-cropped Afro, pencil-thin arms, and bony face. The word *fragile* came to mind.

I sat down in my armchair and glanced through her intake papers. Twenty-eight years old. Single. Employed as a secretary at a law office. In the section labeled "Major Problems," she wrote in small, constricted script that was dwarfed by the enormity of the page: "Severely depressed. Sometimes suicidal thoughts."

Uh oh, I thought, careful not to convey alarm. I steeled myself for the possibility of an extended session before going home, maybe even an unscheduled trip to the emergency room.

Through sobs, Sabrina told me her story, her voice so low I had to struggle at times to hear her. She grew up with an alcoholic father who terrorized her mother, brother, and herself through most of her childhood. Verbal abuse when he was sober escalated into physical beatings when he stumbled home drunk. As a buffer, the three of them formed an impenetrable bond that insulated them emotionally from his onslaughts. Thankfully, one day he disappeared, never to be heard from again.

Life changed for the better from that day forward, until about a year before I met Sabrina. At that time, her mother was diagnosed with cancer, only to pass away six months later. Soon thereafter, Sabrina's brother lost control of his motorcycle, slammed into a tree, and languished in the University of Virginia hospital before himself dying in October.

After Sabrina finished her story, she gazed at her lap, then met my eyes with a look that communicated a desperate plea for help. I instantly realized that she now presented me with my first critical challenge.

Traditional systems of psychotherapy argue that the therapist's first chore is to build trust. To do so, he or she needs to express empathy, show warmth, give reassurance. The establishment of this bond over time, it is argued, provides the necessary foundation for all future collaborative work.

We in REBT have no quarrel with building trust. But we place a premium on a more profound way to do so. That is, we strive to build a bond by immediately working to uncover the irrational thinking that is at the root of the patient's problems, showing him or her the path to peace of mind, and demonstrating one's own commitment to and competence in bringing about substantial change. We believe that all of this not only serves to build trust, but it also opens the door to quickly start the healing process.

In no way was I baffled about the underlying irrational beliefs that were causing Sabrina's depression. Nor was I confused about the next REBT step to take. What gave me pause was the vulnerability she presented. I thought, *What if I cause her to decompensate by pushing too fast? What if I fail and have to take her to the ER? What if she gets offended and storms out?*

But the anguished look in Sabrina's eyes helped me past these "what if's." I took a deep breath and told myself: *Go for it. All I can do is the best I can do. Do what I know to be right.*

Keeping a close eye on her, I took the plunge. "Look, Sabrina, we've just met and you have no idea if I know what I'm doing. But I do. I'm asking you to trust me enough to participate in a thought experiment that might at first blush sound insensitive. I promise it won't hurt you, and it may very well be of real help. Will you trust me?"

She took a deep breath, raised her shoulders, then slumped as she slowly let out air. "Okay."

I smiled to convey reassurance. "Okay," I said, "please bear with me and do your best to answer this question: what percentage of people do you think have suffered tragedies like yours here in Virginia?"

She thought for a few seconds, the room silent except for the sleet pelting the window. "I don't know. Many, I guess."

"I agree, many, but just take a wild guess. What percentage?"

"Maybe twenty percent."

"Sounds like a pretty good guess to me," I said, my chest burning. "Now, how about in our city?"

"Again, maybe twenty percent."

"I agree. Now, lastly, how about in your neighborhood?"

"At least some."

I kept a close watch on Sabrina during this interchange. I neither wanted to anger her nor push her deeper into despair. What I wanted to do was give her hope by helping her identify and release the death grip that her yet-to-be realized irrational belief had on her. Thankfully, she held her jaw steady, kept eye contact with me, and spoke without wavering or weeping.

Just at that moment, a gust of wind rattled the windowpane and the lights flickered. She snapped her head toward the window and then back to me, her eyes wide and her body taut.

"Don't worry, Sabrina," I said, "it's just the wind. You're perfectly safe here. Okay?"

"Okay," she said, forcing a slight, closed-lip smile.

"Ready to go on?"

When she nodded, I said: "Sabrina, you're doing great. Thank you for participating so courageously. Now, please hang in there for another minute or so because we're getting close to beginning to get you better. Yes?"

"Yes."

"Great. Now put on your thinking cap and answer this: What do you think I've been driving at with my questions?"

Sabrina dropped her chin to her chest and studied her hands, clasped tight in her lap. Then she looked back at me and said, "You're trying to get me to see that I'm being selfish."

"Good Lord, no," I shot back. "I'd never think of you as selfish, nor would I ever want you to think that of yourself. Please try again."

She reflected a few seconds and then said, "I'm thinking that I'm a special case."

Excellent, she got it, I thought, as a sense of relief and triumph washed over me. We know that there are two types of depression, each caused by a particular irrational thought. One type is what we call Self-Damning Depression, that is, depression created by a person who believes he or she to be a loser, no good, worthless. The second type is called Catastrophizing Depression, which I knew to be causing Sabrina to feel so despondent. In this type of depression, the person judges the unwanted events in one's life to be so horrible that he or she should not have to bear such a fate.

While gratified by Sabrina's comment, I knew I needed to deepen her insight without going too far too fast. *Be careful,* I cautioned myself. I then asked, "So, Sabrina, when you say you think you're special, what do you mean by that?"

"I guess I'm feeling sorry for myself, thinking it's not fair that this horrible thing has happened to me."

All right! I thought.

This thin, frail woman sitting in front of me, whose voice was so low at the beginning of our conversation that I could barely hear her, had just faced full-on the cause of her depression. Now my chore was to make sure she grasped the importance and power of what she had just said.

"Look, Sabrina," I said, leaning forward, "you've just hit the nail smack dab on its head. You've been through an awful lot—one tragic blow on top of another, ones that would send most anybody reeling. But, if you let yourself think that way—*It's not fair … It shouldn't have happened to me … Life is so horrible I'll never be happy again … I can't bear to live with this*—you'll stay depressed forever."

"But that's the way I feel."

"I get that. But, listen, it's not how you feel, it's the way you're thinking. And that's what's driving your depression. Look, what you start with is quite a normal way of thinking: 'I love my family, sorely miss them, and would give anything to have them back.' That thinking is healthy and causes you to feel the appropriate pain of grief. But you're adding to that the kind of thinking that would make anybody profoundly depressed: 'It's so horrible that it shouldn't have happened to me.' That's what's doing you in. If we can get you to give up that kind of thinking, you'll still love your family and grieve for them, but you won't experience such profound depression that you'll feel you have no hope and want to end your life. Will you work with me on that? What do you say?"

"I say, yes, I will."

And Sabrina did. Within a few months of hard work, she endorsed an anti-catastrophizing way of thinking and thereby clawed her way out of her depression. In her last session, she told me: "I'll hate losing my mother and brother the rest of my life. But what happened, happened. I can either wail against it or I can accept it and do what I can to live a fulfilled life. I choose the latter."

Hearing this, I wanted to give her a hug. But I settled for a warm smile and a "That's wonderful, Sabrina."

Reflection

Would that all of us possessed the courage of Sabrina. But the real message of this chapter is not about her. Rather, it's that anyone who wishes to provide psychotherapy for another human being must do so without succumbing to fear. Of course, use good judgment, exercise prudence, embrace humility. But, take great care to serve your patient's needs without fear of failure, disapproval, or discomfort.

How to do this? It starts with being aware of when you feel fearful. To this day, I still remember the burning sensation in my chest early in Sabrina's first session when I faced the decision whether to play it safe by merely comforting her, or to take the bold leap into addressing her depression-causing irrational thinking.

Not paying attention to that fear could have left me vulnerable to acting on it, to this young lady's long-term detriment. But it goes deeper than that. As those of us who practice REBT know, the most significant value of being attuned to our negative feelings is that they signal that we have adopted an irrational thought which leads to them. Knowing this, we can ferret out that thought and take constructive action to eliminate and replace it.

I think back to the moment when my fear spiked, when I thought, *What if I cause her to decompensate? What if I fail? What if she gets offended?* These thoughts flashed through my mind, not in complete sentences, but as shorthand notions. Nevertheless, I instantly grasped their content:

1. I must be right and perfect in everything I do with Sabrina. To do otherwise would be horrible and shameful of me.
2. I must conduct this session in such a way that there is no pain and discomfort for both her and me. To do otherwise would be horrible and unbearable.

Psychotherapeutic lore says that insight into one's irrational thinking is in and of itself curative of fear (as well as all other emotional problems). Indeed, many techniques employed by those who hold to this premise are used for that very reason—free association, dream analysis, exploring slips of the tongue, analyzing feelings the patient projects onto the therapist, digging up childhood experiences.

We now know that this is simply not so. While insight may be necessary, it is not sufficient. Whether the symptomology be fear or another debilitative emotional state, what is needed is a thorough, sustained working-through process. This means in REBT to repeatedly show ourselves (and, of course, our patients) how illogical, inconsistent with reality, and self-defeating these fear-producing beliefs are, and then re-indoctrinate ourselves (and our patients) with more rational ones that lead to a better emotional outcome.

I had no time to do this in the midst of my charged initial conversation with Sabrina. As a stopgap, I did my best at the moment to swat away those fear-provoking assertions with positive self-talk: *All I can do is my best. Do what I know to be right. Nothing horrible will happen. We'll get through this.*

Thankfully, my decision to cut right to Sabrina's core irrational thinking worked out even better than I had hoped. She embraced the ABCs of REBT, worked diligently to disassociate herself from her catastrophizing thinking, and strove to endorse the more realistic beliefs that washed away her depression. There is no way I could have helped her recover without her courageous efforts. At the same time, there is no way she could have rid herself of her depression had I not defeated my fears and plunged forward as I did.

But it doesn't stop with we psychotherapists merely coping with fear as it arises. The bottom line is that we must adopt the same fearlessness beliefs that we strive to instill in our patients. For, in every session, with every patient, there is always the possibility of failure, disapproval, and discomfort. "Doctor, first heal thyself" is not a bad maxim.

With kudos to the great American psychologist, Dr. Albert Ellis,[1] listed below are the main reasons why the beliefs behind both fears of failure and fears of discomfort are irrational.

With regard to Fears of Failure, I refer you to Chapter 5 in this book, Destroy Self-Esteem, for a fuller discussion. Nevertheless, briefly stated, thinking that one must always do perfectly well or else they become a failure is irrational for the following reasons:

- Nobody, absolutely nobody, can be all competent and masterful. Being human and fallible, everyone must possess weaknesses, have faults, and regularly make errors of one kind or another. This, alas, is the human condition. To expect otherwise of oneself, and, worse, to damn oneself for such imperfections, is to invite a life filled with anxiety, guilt, and depression.
- A person is not definable. You are not what you do (e.g., psychologist, vegetarian, basketball player). You are not the qualities you possess (e.g., curiousity, adventuresome, athletic), nor are you the roles that you play (e.g., husband, father, friend). You are, if anything, a person who does these things and has these qualities. How can someone who is indefinable to begin with ever be rated as entirely good or bad?
- Even if you could define, rate, or judge yourself by a single trait, it would be a gross overgeneralization. Would you demolish your whole house because of a basement leak? Would you junk your car because of a faulty spark plug? Of course not. But that's what you do when you judge yourself as all bad or worthless because of a particular poor performance or a failure.
- A person is an ever-changing process that exists over a long period of time. To define and rate that person at any given time for some particular act or trait is as illogical as taking a snapshot of that person and exclaiming that this one-second image represents his or her whole life.
- Although doing well and being looked upon favorably may be of great benefit on a practical level, connecting one's worth to these outcomes can lead to a life of unnecessary unhappiness. For, by adopting this belief, if one fails to do well and gain approval, one will assuredly experience shame, guilt, and depression. On the other hand, if one succeeds

and receives kudos, one will be happy only for a brief period of time, then relapse into anxiety, for there is no guarantee of success the next time.

With regard to Fears of Discomfort, while an adversity of any shape and size may be difficult and undesirable, it is hardly awful, horrible, or terrible, because:

- Awful, horrible, and terrible are terms that simply do not reflect reality. The worst some undesirable event can be is one hundred percent bad. For something to qualify as awful, it must exceed one hundred percent bad, that is, be at one hundred and one percent bad, or more. Nothing can be more than one hundred percent of anything, so nothing can be so bad as to warrant the judgment of awful, horrible, or terrible.
- While a few things could be reasonably rated as close to one hundred percent bad (e.g., a nuclear war, death of one's child), most bad things rate way down on the badness scale. They thereby warrant judgments like "undesirable," "dislikable," or "unfortunate" rather than "awful," "horrible," or "terrible."
- Though it is certainly true that hardships of one kind or another make life difficult, they are never understandable or unbearable. In point of fact, we humans can and do bear everything we experience until we die. Then it's a moot point.
- Most hardships and hassles are time-limited. We suffer through them, they end, and then we get on with life as before.
- When someone rates something that is objectively undesirable or bad as "awful," "horrible," or "terrible," he or she is actually saying that, since it is so bad, it should not or must

not exist. Although it can be proven that the despised event is bad, it does not follow that it therefore must not exist.
- Thinking in such catastrophic terms creates a "two for the price of one" situation: (1) there is the original adversity with which to deal; (2) there is the emotional pain one has about it. I call this "bargain basement shopping." Moreover, the more one worries about a potentially bad outcome, the more likely it is that the person will be rattled and make decisions that can make the situation worse than it objectively is.

In knowing the irrationality behind both fear of failure and discomfort, the psychotherapist's goal is to bring to each therapy session the following two fearlessness beliefs:

1. I will do my best to always make the right decisions with each of my patients. But I am only human. I can neither perform perfectly nor work miracles. When I do err or fail, I won't like it, but I'll make sure to learn from it for future benefit, without blaming or damning myself as a bad psychotherapist or, worse, a bad person.
2. I want things to go smoothly and comfortably with each of my patients. But it is highly unlikely that this will always be the case. When difficulties and discomforts do arise, as they inevitably will, I will gracefully accept them as hassles that are part of the process without catastrophizing them as horrors to be avoided at all costs.

These guidelines will lead to the best of both worlds. On the one hand, the psychotherapist stays highly motivated to help each and every patient recover to the fullest. On the other hand, he or she will do so without needlessly infecting oneself with fear.

Note

1 Albert Ellis published hundreds of books, chapters, and papers. The following two references can be as good a resource for developing fearlessness as any: Ellis, A. (1998). *How to Control Your Anxiety Before It Controls You.* New York: Kensington Publishing Corporation; Ellis, A. and Harper, R. A. (1998). *A Guide to Rational Living,* 3rd Rev., N. Hollywood, C.A.: Melvin Powers.

4

INTERPERSONAL INTELLIGENCE[1]

Building the trust and goodwill needed to bring about quality change

What you win with is people.
– Joe Gibbs

When Coach Gibbs said the above, he could have been talking to a psychotherapist, for psychotherapy is an intensely intimate relationship in which trust and goodwill are critical. Only through trust and goodwill can there be the kind of open and honest communication and collaborative and hard-nosed problem solving that will lead to constructive change.

But psychotherapy is not a relationship between peers. It is a hierarchical relationship in which one party, the therapist, holds authority, seeks nothing, and has nothing at risk, whereas the other party, the patient, is a supplicant of sorts, vulnerable, and by definition in need and dependent. Given this inequity, there is an irony: while there is a greater need for the patient to trust the therapist than the other way around, there is much more responsibility on the shoulders of the therapist to build trust than on those of the patient.

I remember my psychotherapy training at The Ohio State University. I would sit knee-to-knee with my patient in a room so small there was only enough space for two chairs, a desk tucked tight into the corner, and a dark brown wooden coffee table with a bouquet of artificial flowers on it. We sat in front of a one-way mirror. Behind this mirror sat my supervisor, notepad in her lap, checking off on a scale from one to five how much empathy I expressed. Occasionally she would utter instructions into a microphone that I could hear through an earpiece:

"Reflect her feelings."

"Put more concern into your voice."

"Make better eye contact."

"A good time to give reassurance."

I learned my lesson well, following the trust-building formula of the day. I showed interest by sustaining eye contact, nodding understandingly, interjecting "um's" and "uh-huh's" that communicated both interest and affirmation. I paid attention to the patient's thoughts and feelings, then summed them up in a reflective statement that captured the patient's experience. I gave needed feedback without sounding critical or attacking.

These interpersonal skills served me well. They helped me build the kind of alliances with my patients I needed to help them work with me to solve their problems.

But the more I practiced and taught REBT, the more I realized that all the interpersonal skills in the world would be rendered phony and perfunctory unless they came from a genuine place from deep inside of the psychotherapist. Consider the following metaphor:

Just as an apple tree cannot produce its fruit unless strong at its trunk and healthy at its roots, so too will a psychotherapist be unable to produce his or her desired fruit unless likewise possessing a strong trunk and, especially, a healthy root system (see Figure 4.1.).

For the psychotherapist, the fruit we seek is trust and goodwill. To develop this, the psychotherapist certainly needs to possess the requisite means to do so at his or her trunk. These means include the type of skills I was taught as a graduate student:

INTERPERSONAL INTELLIGENCE 59

Figure 4.1 The tree of producing extraordinary trust and goodwill

sound listening, empathic understanding, and unconditional acceptance.

Yet there are untold numbers of psychotherapists who possess all the interpersonal skills, yet act them out in such a stilted, mechanical way that they still have a difficult time building the trust and goodwill they need in their patients. Why? Because they are deficient or defective at their roots, that is, at the level of their Interpersonal Intelligence. Interpersonal Intelligence thus involves much more than forcing a warm smile onto one's face, vocalizing pat responses, or engaging in verbal sleights-of-hand. Rather, it involves developing deep beliefs, perspectives, or paradigms that prompt the expression of caring, concern, and compassion from deep inside as a byproduct of one's core values.

In what follows, I will flesh out what I believe to be the three most important traits of character and personality that psychotherapists high in Interpersonal Intelligence possess. They are: (1) Premeditated Acceptance and Forgiveness, (2) Generosity, and (3) Compassion. Using the theory and practice of REBT on oneself, each trait can be endorsed, developed, and used effectively with sustained practice.

Premeditated Acceptance and Forgiveness

Fifty-seven-year-old Greg lumbered into my office wearing baggy gray sweatpants, mud-flecked black sneakers, and an untucked t-shirt embossed with the giant red tongue of Mick Jagger. Taking in his squat stature, lumpy body, and lose unshaven jowls, the word "schlump" came to mind.

He plopped down on the love seat across from me and pulled his right leg up by his ankle, then tucked it under his left thigh with the side of his shoe resting on the couch. Stifling a frown, I scanned his intake information and noted that his major complaint said, "Mood Swings, Especially Anger Issues."

Before I could speak, he scowled at me so that his dark eyebrows nearly touched at the bridge of his nose. He said, "You know I really don't want to be here, don't you?"

A live wire, I thought, instantly recognizing the dreaded trifecta of resistance, confrontiveness, and abrasiveness. Careful to keep my voice calm and level, I said, "Well, I do hear that from patients now and then. That's okay. Why don't you tell me what spurred you to be here despite that."

"My wife," Greg said, spitting the words out like they tasted of vinegar. "She said that if I didn't get help it'd be over between us."

"Well, what are her complaints? Maybe I can help you fix them, maybe not, but unless I know what they are, I for sure won't be able to help. Okay?"

That opened the floodgates. Greg told me about the contentious relationship he had with his wife and their two sons. Almost without taking a breath or pausing between sentences, he gave detailed examples of what he called their rudeness and disrespect. As he talked, he became more and more animated, bouncing in his chair, eyes ablaze, his arms flailing. Despite several attempts, I couldn't interrupt his tirade until he spent himself and slumped back into his seat.

"Wow," I said, moving into true REBT mode, "quite a complicated mess you've got here. But what impresses me is that you've really got two problems, not just one. One is obviously the very conflicted and acrimonious relationship you have with your family. This clearly needs to be cleaned up. The second is the bushel basket of white-hot anger you carry inside you that is, I suspect, what drove your wife to deliver her ultimatum."

Ignoring my last point, Greg bolted upright in his seat and raised his voice almost to a shout. "You're goddamn right I'm angry!"

The image of a charging bull flashed before me. *Keep a cool head*, I told myself before saying, "Lookit, Greg, your family may very well be a royal pain, but surely you can see that your anger is part of the problem. Even if they start every single squabble, your getting angry has got to add fuel to the fire."

While I talked, Greg squirmed in his seat. His eyes darted. He sputtered "but" several times in an attempt to interrupt me. When I finished, he spat out, "But they show me no respect."

I had worked with many angry, argumentative patients before and knew that neither reflecting Greg's feelings nor debating with him would lead to a constructive outcome. I knew that both these tactics would only serve to reinforce the irrational thinking that led to his anger. I chose instead to teach him the ABCs of his anger and illustrated on my whiteboard the vicious circle that operated between him and his family (see Figure 4.2).

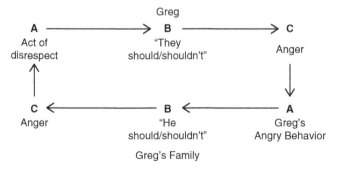

Figure 4.2 Greg and family vicious circle

Without much confidence that this would lead the conversation into a more promising path, I concluded by saying that he could only break this pattern by letting go of his anger.

No sooner had I finished explaining this to Greg, he shot back, "That's too fucking simple."

I could feel the first hints of anger well in my own chest but quickly reminded myself: *Don't take this personal, he's a troubled person.*

Taking in and expelling a deep breath, I then said, "Greg, you're right that all this is simple, but that doesn't mean it's not true. You've got to decide whether or not you're willing to work on fixing the kind of thinking you do that causes your anger, or just go on like this until you end up in divorce court. I'm here to help you do that if you want."

No matter what I said, he responded with "Yeah, but …" insisting that his family caused him to be angry, that they should treat him with the respect he deserved, that the resolution of his family conflicts rested on their shoulders, not his.

I knew this was leading nowhere constructive. After several exchanges, I finally told him that, no matter how much he tried to convince me he was right, his way of thinking would never change his behavior nor that of his family. I emphasized that, since he suffered the problems that brought him to my office, the only hope he had was to put debating on hold and instead take a hard-nosed, critical look at his own pattern of thinking. Only by doing that could he ever hope to ever repair his family relationships.

Before I even got the last sentence out of my mouth, he jumped to his feet, glared down at me, and yelled, "Fuck you then!" With that he stormed out of my office, slamming the door so hard the walls rattled.

I sat for a few minutes, taking deep breaths, letting my heartbeat calm. Just as I was about to walk to my desk to prepare for my next patient, the door quietly opened and Greg stuck his head in. "Can I come back?" he asked, then added, "I've done that more times than I can count. And I know I can't afford to keep doing it."

"Good," I said. "Glad you came back. Have a seat and let's try again to get on the same page."

With what could only be described as an embarrassed grin, Greg said, "Okay Doc."

Reflection

I would love to report that from that moment forward Greg transformed into the cooperative, motivated patient we psychotherapists all covet. From an REBT standpoint, that would mean that he fully appreciated that the cost of his anger far outweighed its advantages, accepted full and total responsibility for bringing his anger onto himself rather than blaming it on his family, and worked to identify, debunk, and replace his anger-creating irrational thinking.

Alas, that was not to be, nor did I expect him to undergo such a complete transition. For weeks he continued to resist my ministrations, sometimes listening, but, as often as not, debating, advocating for the validity of his irrational thinking, sometimes showing flashes of anger. To this day, he occasionally still does this, but these episodes now come infrequently and are easily deflected.

What saved the day with this difficult patient? Simple. Patience and persistence, fueled by a healthy dose of the Interpersonal Intelligence trait of Premeditated Acceptance and Forgiveness. In REBT terms, this means that I kept front and center in my mind the following rational principles whenever I sat with Greg:

1. All Patients Are Imperfect. This may seem obvious, but it is worth emphasizing that no patient is a saint or an angel. Being a fallible human being, and most likely a troubled one at that, he or she will inevitably bring quirks, idiosyncrasies, and sometimes even quite obnoxious behaviors into the clinical office. As it was for me with Greg, a therapist will at times face resistance, impatience, laziness, irritability, and even unreasonable, insensitive, and rude behavior. Rather than demand that your patient always act cooperatively and respectfully, remember that he or she must act contrary at times. The question is not whether you'll confront this, but when. So what!

2. Take Nothing Personal. Never take anything a patient does or says personally. How he or she acts—good, bad, indifferent, even when aimed directly at you—is a reflection of that person's current state of mind. It is not about you or against you. I can't begin to count the number of times I applied these thoughts to Greg: *Remember, he's a troubled person. Given the irrational ways of thinking he's engrained over a lifetime, he must act that way. Just hang in there with him.*

3. Never Judge. REBT is a pioneer in preaching the importance of separating what people do from who they are. Simply said, there are no entirely good or entirely bad people, only fallible humans, who do both good and bad things. While acceptable and sometimes desirable to judge people's actions, it is never appropriate to judge them as all good or all bad.

As I try to do with all my patients, I did my best with Greg to follow the wisdom of Mother Theresa: "If you judge people, you have no time to love them." I can remember telling myself on many occasions such things as: "He can't help acting this way." "He means well, though he easily gets caught up in his nutty thinking." "He's a fallible human being just doing the best he can." My self-talks were hardly as eloquent as Mother Theresa's words, but they helped me forgive and accept Greg as I confronted his difficult behavior.

Generosity

More than a few Decembers ago, my wife and I took our son Gabriel to see a stage production of *A Christmas Carol*, the story of Ebenezer Scrooge, a bitter, lonely miser who only cares about money and who treats people without compassion or warmth. To him, people only matter as commodities, their only purpose to do his bidding and increase his wealth.

The dramatic center of this tale takes place on Christmas Eve when three ghosts visit him as he sleeps. The Ghost of Christmas Past shows him scenes of his youth when he and his family reveled in the warmth and happiness that no longer is his. The Ghost of Christmas Present takes him to the family Christmas celebration of one of his employees, Bob Cratchit. He and his family bathe in their love for one another despite the impending death of their beloved son, Tiny Tim. The Ghost of Christmas Future transports him to his own gravesite where no one is present to remember or care that he ever lived.

The intervention works. Scrooge recognizes the waste and barrenness of his life. Awakening on Christmas Day, he bounds out of bed a newborn man. With joy in his heart and a smile on his face, he races out his front door and every person he meets he sees as an opportunity to make their life nicer, warmer, richer. He is transformed into a living, breathing font of generosity.

Reflection

The spirit of generosity. What a wonderful perspective to bring into the psychotherapy office. Imagine the trust and goodwill we'd earn with our patients by being generous with our time, attention, and patience. Imagine the trust and goodwill we'd create by choosing to leave no patient encounter without showing some small act of generosity. Imagine the sense of satisfaction we'd feel at the end of the day.

It takes so little time and energy to act with generosity. I think of the mother, denied access to her children by Social Services due to her severe alcoholism. When I called to deliver the message from her sons that they loved her, she cried and said, "God bless you, Dr. Grieger." I think of the twenty-something young man who hugged me for the letter of support I gave to the court on the day of his trial for drug use. I think of the indigent elderly woman who wept when I waived the insurance co-payment she couldn't afford.

Generosity is more a gift of self than a tangible act. With the right principles rooted in one's belief system, acts of generosity blossom naturally without forethought or planning. Here then are three principles that I have found useful in keeping the spirit of generosity alive and well in my office.

1. People Value Being Valued. Though being valued may not be an absolute human need, all people do treasure it. Perceiving oneself as valued warms the heart, uplifts the spirit, stokes trust and goodwill. What better way to communicate to another person that they are valued than to act generously toward them.

2. The Little Things Are the Big Things. A warm greeting, a word of encouragement, a pat on the back can mean as much or more to someone than a gifted object. Why? Because these small acts communicate acceptance to those who may not accept themselves, kindness to those who feel estranged from affection, comfort to those suffering emotional pain, a reminder that there is goodness in the world to those who have not experienced much of it in their lives.

3. Opportunities Abound. As with Ebenezer Scrooge, every encounter we have with another person provides an opportunity to act generously. Reminding oneself to devote full attention to the patient who verbalizes the same irrational thinking for the fiftieth time is an apt example. So is giving your private cell phone number to a patient in crisis, or taking pains to return a patient's phone calls in a timely manner. Opportunities do abound. All you have to do is be alert to them.

Compassion

I expected this to be a routine marriage counseling case when Daryl and Heather first walked into my office. Mid-to-late thirties, a little overweight, they each greeted me with a half-smile and a handshake. Daryl stood about six feet tall, had broad shoulders and short light brown hair. The glide in his walk made me wonder if he had played linebacker for his college football team. Heather wore her raven hair straight, falling to her shoulders. She had squeezed into tight jeans, above which she wore a baggy sweater that hung down over her hips. Fur-topped boots that came to mid-calf completed the picture of a down-to-earth woman comfortable with herself in all situations.

What could be their problem? I wondered, then blanched when I saw what they had written for their reason for seeking help: "Son Justin's death."

They poured out their anguish, Heather doing most of the talking, her words coming out raw between sobs, without a hint of self-consciousness or apology. About two months before, their sweet, good-looking, sixteen-year-old Justin, a life-long epileptic, had a seizure while alone in his bedroom. His heart just stopped. SUDEP, it's called, Sudden Unexpected Death in Epilepsy without an anatomical cause. Daryl found him on his bedroom floor when returning home for lunch.

No training prepares a psychotherapist for such a moment. Feeling stunned, I mustered a pitiful, "I'm so sorry." Then I said, "This may sound a bit absurd, but can you tell me how you're reacting to your loss?"

That's when Daryl jumped in: "We're lost and don't know what to do. I can compartmentalize my feelings and sometimes have a normal day. But forget about me. Right now I'm worried about Heather."

Turning to her, I said, "Can you tell me how you're doing?"

"Not good."

"Well, I can imagine your profound sense of grief. But do you experience anything else besides grief that also pains you?"

"Guilt, terrible guilt."

"I'm sorry," I said, "but why do you feel so guilty?"

"It's so unfair. He suffered from seizures his whole life, always worrying about another one coming on, the social stigma and all. Then for this to happen to him, all alone." She dabbed her eyes, then went on. "I should have been there for him that morning. I should have researched SUDEP more instead of stupidly reassuring him that the worst thing that'll ever happen is that he'll have another seizure. I should have done something to save him."

With that, Heather sobbed, her hands covering her face, her body convulsing. Daryl pulled her into his arms and stroked her hair.

"It's okay," I said. "Take your time. I understand."

I waited without speaking as Heather cried herself out. Glancing at the clock, I saw that it was just a few minutes before noon, but pushed the thought out of my mind to end the session for lunch.

After a while, Heather sat up and looked at me with red-rimmed eyes and mascara-streaked cheeks. In a soft voice without adornment, she spoke her bottom-line truth: "I don't know how I can live without him. I've lost my reason for living."

In classic REBT, we psychotherapists systematically teach the patients the fundamentals of self-therapy so that they can practice it on their own. We first help them see and appreciate the irrational beliefs that spawn their self-imposed suffering. In this case, it was Heather's guilt, despondency, and anger on top of her profound grief. Then we systematically lead the patient through a logical and empirical analysis of their irrational thinking, until they see these thoughts as untrue. In the final step, we teach patients to re-indoctrinate themselves with sensible, rational beliefs that relieve their symptomatic pain.

Right then and there I knew that this was not the time to do classic REBT. I needed to provide guidance and direction. I could fill in the blanks later.

Putting as much conviction and authority into my voice as I could, I said, "Heather, Daryl, we have just met, but, if you'll trust me, there's every reason to believe you'll get through this. What do you say?"

"Please help us," Heather said, pleading.

"Go for it, Doc," Daryl added.

"Okay, then," I said, "let's get started. I want to offer you two things before you leave today. They won't immediately help you, but I promise they will over time, and maybe not as far off in the future as you think. There's hope. Okay?"

"Okay," Daryl said. Heather nodded.

I leaned forward, shortening the distance between us, looking back and forth from one to the other. "First, I want you to know, really know, that most of what you're feeling is normal. You're not crazy. You're supposed to feel this pain. Any normal person who's just lost his or her son is going to be devastated. I know I would. This may sound stupid, but, by accepting your pain as normal, it will not be so bad for you. It's when people tell themselves that they shouldn't have it, that they can't bear it, that it'll never get better, that's when it feels unbearable. In a sense, if you'll just let yourself have it, not fight it, or catastrophize it, it will begin to lessen."

I paused, letting this sink in. Then I said, "Now, having said that, I want to make a second point. We need to make a distinction between your grief and your guilt, depression, and anger.

While I want you to let yourself just accept your grief as normal and trust that time will take care of it, I want to help you be rid of all the rest of your pain—that anger, guilt, and depression. Let me give you an example of how I defeated these latter feelings when my dad died. I want you to know that I don't compare the loss of my dad with your loss, but I think you can benefit from my experience."

Years before, my dad died unexpectedly one spring night when I was flying home for a long weekend visit. When my taxi pulled up in front of my house, I found my mother standing on the front lawn with her three sisters.

Seeing me, she practically shouted, "Your dad just died," and rushed to embrace me.

Mom and I spent a sleepless night in the living room, alternatively crying and reminiscing. The next morning, alone, I realized I had to be strong both for her as well as for myself. Before I went to the funeral home to make the necessary arrangements, I sat down with paper and pencil at the dining room table, where my family had shared untold numbers of meals. I wrote out for myself a series of rational thoughts that I hoped would prevent me from descending into my own depression and bitterness. I vowed to meditate on these rational thoughts three times a day for the next six months to keep myself sane and functional.

Here are the rational thoughts I wrote that morning:

- My dad is now peaceful and happy. If there is a God, he is with him in heaven, not suffering, grateful to be where he is, and not depressed because he is not on this earth. Be pleased for him.
- My dad loved me all my life. He wanted me to be happy while he lived and he surely would want me to be happy in my life now. Don't betray his wishes.

- Dad's life was shorter than he or I would have liked, but it was still rich in love and adventure. It wasn't the years in his life that mattered, but the life in his years. Be happy for this.
- While I now feel the profound pain of grief, I can and will bear it until it lessens and eventually goes away. This pain is part of life. Accept it without protest.
- I'd give anything to have my dad back with me. But I don't need him to be here. I can and will survive and eventually thrive despite the loss of him. Be confident in that.
- While I will miss my dad for the rest of my life, my life contains more than just him. I can grieve for him while appreciating and taking pleasure from what still exists in my life, despite this loss. Be happy for what you still have.
- My dad had to die—how he did and when he did. All the conditions were present for him to die and none were present to prevent him from dying. No matter how much I hate this fact, he absolutely should or must have died that night. Accept it without blame or bitterness.

All this I shared with Heather and Daryl. I urged them to do what I did—meditate on the same or similar thoughts about the loss of their son several times a day for the next several months.

"Will you do that?" I asked. "It probably won't help immediately, but I predict you'll find relief in due time."

"Will you write it out for us?" Daryl asked.

"You bet. But will you follow through?"

"I will," he said.

"Heather?"

"I will."

"Yeah?"

"Yeah."

Reflection

Daryl, Brandy, and I met weekly for three months. They each meditated on their rational thinking between sessions, while I pecked away at the irrationality of their beliefs face-to-face. I was so happy to see them embrace this process. I cherish the memory of our last appointment when Brandy hugged me and said, "I still have my bad days, but, thanks to you, I have my life back."

Like with all my patients, I know that I am powerless to bring about change in them. All my insights and skills, rounded and honed over thirty-five years of experience, are useless unless embraced and used by them. Daryl and Heather made the commitment to work to endorse the ways of thinking that allowed them to gracefully accept the pain of their grief and to shed the soul-crushing anguish of guilt, depression, and anger.

Yet I do pride myself for the compassion I brought to each and every minute I spent with them. More than active listening, compassion is a willingness to extend one's self to another for their benefit. In the first conversation with Daryl and Heather, I gave them my full attention, all the time they needed, and, maybe most importantly, a personal experience from my life. I have to think that these acts of compassion helped build the trust that in turn allowed me to be of service to them.

From what the ABCs of REBT communicate, acts of compassion (at C) come naturally when one lives by the beliefs (at B) that spawn them. Here are three core beliefs that can make compassion a staple of every psychotherapist's box of tools.

1. People Hunger for Compassion. Compassion is perhaps the greatest gift one can give to another. Why? Because it's a gift of self. When treated with compassion, no one, except perhaps the most hardened psychopath, can resist feeling warm toward the giver and wanting to give back.

2. A Hard Day's Night. No one's life is free of hardships or hassles. The gamut runs from minor setbacks to profound tragedies. The point is that everybody struggles with life and has hard days. Once one appreciates this, acts of compassion can come naturally.

3. It Rewards the Giver. What goes around comes around. By communing with people from a place of compassion, the experience of practicing psychotherapy is transformed from simply plying one's craft into an intimate connection between two or more people. The patient benefits, but so too does the psychotherapist.

Final Reflection

Stephen Covey captured it best: "Trust is the glue that binds people together."[2] Without trust, there is little hope that two people will work harmoniously together to create cherished goals. With it, there can be goodwill, cooperation and collaboration, the opportunity to produce something no one person could accomplish by himself or herself alone.

But trust is not a birthright. It is something that has to be earned. It develops over time when one acts in a trustworthy way. It comes from two necessary sources: one's competence and one's character. By the psychotherapist behaving competently, the patient can come to believe that the psychotherapist has the skills to help the patient resolve his or her personal issues. By the psychotherapist behaving with sound character, the patient can feel comfortable in letting his or her guard down and opening up to what the psychotherapist has to offer.

The bottom line is that one's character is defined by the core principles a person holds and acts on across situations. Those core principles necessary to build trust and goodwill I group under the term Interpersonal Intelligence. They are: (1) Premeditated Acceptance and Forgiveness, (2) Generosity, and (3) Compassion. Trustworthy behavior bubbles up naturally from the inside out when a psychotherapist embodies these. I urge all who wish to provide psychotherapy to others to steep themselves in each of these principles.

Notes

1 I first introduced the concept of Interpersonal Intelligence in chapter 5 of my book, *Developing Unrelenting Drive, Dedication, and Determination*, published by Routledge in 2017.
2 See Stephen H. Covey's masterpiece, *The 7 Habits of Highly Effective People*, published by Simon and Schuster, pages 188–203.

5

DESTROY SELF-ESTEEM

Self-esteem is the problem,
not the solution

*The privilege of a lifetime
is being who you are.*
— Joseph Campbell

Of the thousands of disturbed people I've treated, a disproportionately high number became so because they esteemed themselves in a negative light. I think of Betty, trapped in a marriage to an abusive husband because of her conviction that to fail in her relationship with him would prove that she was the unlovable person she secretly believed herself to be. Then there was Sam, he with a hair-trigger temper, spurred by his assumption that any slight denigrated his worth as a man. I think of Julie and Lauren and Heather, three women rejected by their mothers, who were so desperate to feel good about themselves that they sacrificed their own desires in desperate attempts to succor favor and gain self-worth.

But one need look no further than my experience in the spring of 1973 to appreciate the ravages of self-esteem. One Wednesday evening sitting with thousands of others in the McLeod Hall auditorium on the grounds of the University of Virginia, I waited for the famed anthropologist, Dr. Margaret Mead. She was to deliver the keynote address to open the School of Medicine's conference on "The Legitimacy of Behavior Control." The next morning, I was scheduled to be one of five presenters whose remarks she was to critique. I would then be a panelist with her in the afternoon session.

At exactly eight o'clock, the door at the back of the auditorium clanged open and Margaret Mead marched down the aisle, followed by two tall women in business suits. She looked small and stout, like a fireplug, wore a wool cape that draped to her ankles, and carried a chin-high walking stick that she thumped to the floor with each step. When she passed, she looked directly at me. She had the square head of a bulldog, short gray hair that fit her like a helmet, and eyes behind wire-rim glasses that showed no warmth or mercy.

Feelings of intimidation exploded inside me like a hand grenade the moment Dr. Mead took the stage. While she was introduced by an Associate Dean, she took offense at something he said. Taking the microphone, she cut him to the quick with a retort that brought into question his manhood.

The audience chorused a collective gasp, then settled into an awkward silence.

"Oh, shit," I muttered, realizing I could be on the receiving end of the same treatment the next day should I displease her.

I slept little that night, replaying over and over what I had witnessed earlier. In the dark, untethered from all the trappings of the real world, my mind roamed over imagined scenes of humiliation and horror that might befall me the next day.

I pictured myself standing behind the lectern, my notes scattered in front of me, delivering my brief remarks to the packed crowd. In my mind, I make it through my speech, gather my notes, and return to my chair to polite applause. Margaret Mead remains seated until the room quietens, then gathers herself to her full height of five feet in front of her chair. She does not walk to the lectern but stares at me without expression before turning to the audience. I hold my breath, feeling like I'm in a courtroom, about to hear my fate from a jury foreman. After what seems like an eternity, Dr. Mead stomps her walking stick to the floor with a thud that booms as if she has shot off a cannon. Pointing at me, she says to the audience, "That was the biggest bunch of claptrap I've ever heard. This young man shouldn't be allowed to clean this university's toilets much less hold a faculty position."

Some in the audience gasp, their hands over their mouths. Others just stare. I sit stunned, frozen. I feel exposed as a lightweight, a sham, a dunce. I imagine myself so nervous that sweat colors my clothing, coherent speaking impossible.

As I pictured this scene, nothing could distract me from such horror—not meditation, rational thinking, or prayer. Fear escalated into panic, then turned into fantasies of escape. Could I feign sickness? Say one of my parents had died? What about simply not showing up?

Eight o'clock the next morning, I stumbled into my office. On the outside I looked buttoned-up and put-together—clean-shaven, professional in my dark blue suit, shoes polished to a sparkle. On the inside, though, I was a mess, not only scared of my fate at the hands of Margaret Mead, but also terrified that I might humiliate myself in public.

I looked at my wristwatch: eight-thirty. This was it. I had to be on-stage and ready to go at nine. With a deep sigh, I stood up to leave. Just then my office door opened and one of my friends stuck his head in. "How're you doing?" he asked.

"Not so hot," I said. "I'm pretty much a basket case."

"I figured," he said. "Here, I've got something that will help." In one hand, he held a light blue pill, a cup of Coke in the other.

"What's this?"

"Xanax," he said. "By the time you get to the auditorium, you'll feel as content as a baby sucking on a Binky."

I swallowed the pill and, when I walked onto the stage at McLeod Hall twenty minutes later, I felt gathered and peaceful. When I introduced myself to Margaret Mead, I chuckled at how diminutive she looked. Then I took my seat among my fellow panelists in a row of chairs stage right, a lectern positioned to our left. Several thousand people sat in rows in front of me, scattered among them a few of my students and friends. My pill-supplier caught my eye and gave me the thumbs-up sign. I nodded and smiled.

The program began. Each panelist made a twenty-minute presentation followed by Margaret Mead who contributed her comments. My presentation, titled "The Natural Laws of Behavior Modification," was third. With a silent thank-you to the wonders of chemicals, I delivered my presentation coherently, after which Dr. Mead made a few inconsequential comments.

That afternoon we all sat on stage in a semi-circle facing the audience, Margaret Mead in the middle. After she spoke, she invited the audience to ask anything they wanted of us. For close to an hour and a half, people peppered her with questions. The only one not asked of her was directed to me. It had to do with the techniques of behavior modification, which I fielded without a stumble, then settled back into the shadow of the great one.

Near the end of the afternoon's program, I glanced to my right at Margaret Mead three chairs down from me. She looked even smaller than she did that morning, her face slack from the rigors of the day. I scanned the audience, mostly strangers, who didn't matter to me, nor I to them. Surprise and self-disdain washed through me, preceded by the thought, *What an idiot I was to put myself through that ordeal.*

And that, dear reader, was as painful a moment as I ever want to experience. In hindsight, what I did to bring it on was to believe that my self-worth was in jeopardy. I believed that, if I failed at the conference, I would forever be a failure.

You clinicians will surely recall the many patients you've treated who've shared experiences similar to mine. And I suspect that you non-clinicians will also remember times when you endured the same ego-driven panic I did, maybe before an academic test or job interview, perhaps when preparing that first holiday meal for in-laws, or possibly when you thought you might have failed with the person you loved.

In REBT, we take what many think to be a sacrilegious approach to treating self-esteem problems. Instead of helping patients shore up their lagging self-esteem, we consciously and purposely go about the process of destroying the concept of self and the allegiance to self-esteem itself.

To illustrate how this plays out in REBT, let me take you back to my clinical office. Imagine that I, Dr. Grieger, will treat a new patient, Russ, who recently experienced a troubling anxiety episode involving the famed anthropologist, Margaret Mead. Trust that this imaginary first session realistically portrays the hundreds of such sessions I've conducted over the years. With this hypothetical first session, I hope to answer the following three questions: (1) What exactly is this concept called self-esteem? (2) Why is the concept both fallacious and pernicious? (3) What is the alternative to self-esteem that can rid the person of anxiety, depression, and guilt, once and for all?

After glancing through Russ's intake form, I say, "Tell me about your anxiety episode."

Russ relates the conference story while I make notes about both salient details and clinical speculations. I sum it up to him by saying, "So, you suffered a severe bout of anxiety brought on by the possibility of screwing up at the conference and being criticized by Margaret Mead in front of all those people. Did I get it?"

"Yes," he replies with squinted eyes and a deep breath that tells me he is picturing the same pain he did while in the situation.

"Sorry to make you relive something so unpleasant," I say, "but I need you to stay in that moment a little longer and tell me how you judged the possibility of that happening—good, bad, indifferent."

"That's easy," he replies. "I thought that it would be horrible."

"But by horrible do you mean that the audience might rush the stage and tear you limb from limb? Or did you mean that you'd be reduced, publicly, to some kind of worthless person, a veritable piece of shit."

"The latter," he says without hesitation, a wry smile crossing his face.

There it is, I think, *the twin monsters called self and self-esteem.* I inhibit my desire to rush forward into the metaphysics of both of those concepts, knowing that I have to first ground this young man in the necessary insights before I could commence his cure. To get him started, I draw the ABCs of REBT on the rectangular whiteboard mounted on an easel to the right of my chair (Figure 5.1). I explain to him that it really wasn't the possibility of criticism (at A) that caused his anxiety (at C). Rather, it was the belief he held (at B) that, by virtue of doing poorly and being disapproved of by the people in the audience, he'd be rendered worthless, that is, his self-esteem would be guttered.

While I talk, Russ leans forward, elbows on his knees, chin cupped in the palm of his hands. His eyes travel back and forth between me and the whiteboard.

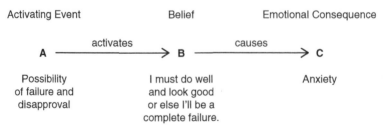

Figure 5.1 Russ's ABCs

"So you're telling me that I brought this anxiety on myself by connecting my self-worth to what might happen at that conference?"

"Exactly!" I say in a strong voice to emphasize my point. "In your mind, you connected your whole worth as a human being to how well you did and how good you looked. No wonder you scared yourself to death, since what you value most, you, was at stake. By virtue of this thinking, you doomed yourself to this severe anxiety."

"Holy shit," he says, his eyes wide.

"Holy shit is right. And, guess what, if you had bombed, you would have replaced your anxiety with shame and depression when walking out of that auditorium. Why? Because, with your self-esteem connected to your performance, you would have thought of yourself as a total failure for having failed. Right?"

"Right," he says, then looks back to the whiteboard.

"That's why, to prevent future anxiety and depression," I say, "we'd better get you to disconnect your self from how well you do and what others think of you."

Russ tilts his head and gives me a quizzical look. "But, if I don't connect my self-esteem to that, from where do I get it?"

"Well, why do you even have to have self-esteem?"

"Why do I even have to have self-esteem? Are you nuts?" he blurts out, more a statement than a question.

"Let me explain what I mean," I say and quote from Jean-Paul Sartre, who famously said in his seminal book on Existentialism, *Being and Nothingness*: "Existence precedes essence" (1956, p. 60). I then draw The Cycle of Life (Figure 5.2) on the whiteboard, and, pointing to the word "Being," go on to explain to Russ that

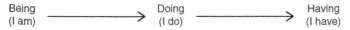

Figure 5.2 The cycle of life

his existence commenced on the sixth day of February, 1942. At that moment, he became a Being, a Self, simple and undifferentiated to be sure, but one nevertheless. If he then had the capacity to answer the question, "Who are you?" he would have simply said, "I am." He would not have qualified that with adjectives, such as "I am a human being," "I am a baby," or "I am a boy." No, he would have just answered, "I am."

I pause to let this sink in, then go on to say that, from this initial state of Being, he started Doing. Early on, he could only do vegetative things—sleeping, crying, digesting. Gradually, as he matured, his Doing became more complicated and sophisticated. Crawling turned into walking and then into running; his guttural sounds evolved into words and then grew into thoughts and concepts; at first he merely looked at people, then smiled at them, and finally interacted socially with them. On and on it went as he passed through Little League baseball, high school and college, and then into his career. I emphasized that it was the "I am" that did all those things, starting at the inception of his Being and continuing to this very day.

"Okay so far?" I ask.

He nods and I go on to tell him that out of his Doing then came his Having. He came to have all his inner or personal qualities—his character traits, his hopes and dreams, his sense of humor, his IQ, his values, his feelings. He came to have all the roles he plays—son, brother, friend, psychologist, husband, and father. He came to acquire and have all his possessions—his house, bank account, car, clothing, friends, enemies, and on and on.

"So, Russ," I say, pointing to the whiteboard, "the Cycle of Life goes from Being to Doing and then to Having. It's a one-way street, left to right. But, to create your anxiety, what you did was pervert the Cycle of Life by going backwards. You made two serious errors. First, you defined who you are, your Being or your

Self, by what you Do, for example, by your performance at this conference, and by what you Have, in this case the approval or lack thereof of others."

I pause to make sure he and I are on the same page. "Okay?" I ask.

When he again nods, I go on to tell him that he also made a second error. After defining himself by what he did and had, he followed that by rating, judging, or esteeming his Being or Self as all good or all bad by whether he performed well or badly and whether or not people gave him their approval.

"Wow," Russ says, eyes wide and mouth open.

"Wow is right." I say. "So, let's play with these two conceptual errors for a minute. Okay? Let me ask you, Are you a man?"

"Yes, of course."

"No, that's not correct," I say. "You're a Being that has the gender of male.

Man would be a quality you have and goes under Having, not Being. Right?"

"Okaaay," he says, drawing the word out quizzically.

"Well, then, are you a university professor?"

"No, I guess not."

"Why not?"

He pauses, then says, "I do professoring a lot of the time, say from 9:00 am to 5:00 pm, Monday through Friday. But it's what I do, not who I am. Did I get it right?"

"You did," I say. "Professoring would go under Doing, not Being. And, by the way, you do all sorts of other things, don't you—listen to music, exercise, talk to your wife, read books, and on and on. So, you do all those things, but you are not any one or even all of them."

I sit there quietly, as does he, both of us studying The Cycle of Life on the whiteboard. I wait for this new paradigm to sink into his consciousness.

Finally he looks at me and asks, "Well, then, Dr. Grieger, who am I?"

I smile at him, careful not to look patronizing. "Great question, exactly the one to ask," I say. "If you're not bored yet with my illustrations, let me help you answer that question by drawing yet another figure on the board, The Circle and Dots" (Figure 5.3).

I explain to Russ that the circle represents his Being or Self, the dots all the millions of his Doings and Havings over the course of his lifetime. I then offer him two choices with regard to the answers to his question of who he is:

- The first one, which most people adopt, contains the twin perversions of defining one's Self by arbitrarily selected Do's or Have's and then esteeming one's Self as all good or all bad by virtue of how well one rates those Do's and/or Have's. This is what we call *Self-Esteem*.
- The second choice is the one championed by REBT. We call this *Unconditional Self-Acceptance*. In it, we neither define nor esteem one's Self at all. I exist, I am. While I do all these dots and have all these other dots, I stubbornly refuse to either define myself or rate myself as all good or bad by any one dot, collection of dots, or even all my dots. Instead, I will

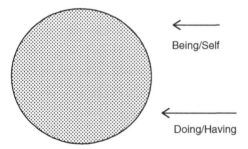

Figure 5.3 The circle and dots

intelligently rate or esteem how well I do and the quality of my haves, which will aid and abet my ongoing potential for happiness and productivity. But I will never define or rate my whole Self. I give up self and self-esteem entirely.

Somewhat spent from the energy I put into this conversation, I lean back in my chair, take a deep breath, and sigh. "Your choice, Russ," I say, "what's it going to be?"

He looks at me, a big grin spreading across his face. "I get it, Doc."

"Yeah, what?"

"I got that who I am is nothing, and how can nothing be bad."

My smile matches his. I feel pleased with his new understandings—that self-esteem is an invalid and pernicious concept he'd best rid from his mind, and that he must replace it with the new paradigm of Unconditional Self-Acceptance. I know there is more work to do, as this insight, though necessary for change, is not sufficient. I'm eager to push forward, as I hope he is.

Reflections

Years ago, John Boyd and I wrote a book titled *Rational-Emotive Therapy: A Skills-Based Approach* (1980). In it, we describe the practice of REBT as a four-step sequential process: Step One: psychodiagnosis; Step Two: patient insight; Step Three: disputational working through; and Step Four: cognitive-philosophical re-education.

Over the years, I've come to appreciate that, while steps one and two are necessary, steps three and four constitute the heart of the REBT change process. It is in step three that the psychotherapist helps the patients see and understand how irrational are his or her disturbance-producing beliefs. Then, in step four, the psychotherapist assists the patient in endorsing and habituating new rational beliefs, which lead to appropriate, healthy emotional and behavioral reactions.

To orchestrate a patient's paradigm shift from self-esteem to self-acceptance, the psychotherapist must firmly and fully understand how destructive self-esteem can be to a person's mental health and how fallacious a concept it is. For starters, I list below ten ways a person can damage his or her happiness and well-being by esteeming himself or herself poorly. He or she:

1. Will frequently suffer much emotional pain. When approaching a task, he or she will experience severe anxiety because failure may very well be just around the corner. If failure does result, then so will guilt and depression. Why? Because to fail will render that person a worthless failure.
2. Will be prone to outbursts of anger, for, when treated in ways perceived to be rude, inconsiderate, or unfair, he or she may very well interpret it to be an assault on his or her self and act to retaliate in order to re-establish a sense of worth.
3. May become so "needy" of the approval of others in order to feel worthwhile that he or she sacrifices one's own desires or opinion in favor of that of others.
4. May become avoidant across any number of important life arenas—relationship commitments, creative endeavors, public performances, sports efforts, work or academic assignments—in order to protect his or her sense of self-worth from failure. His or her attitude would be: "If I do not risk failure, then I don't risk losing my worth, so why take the chance."
5. Can become perfectionistic, even somewhat obsessive-compulsive, for anything but sterling performance equals failure and hence worthlessness.
6. May sacrifice personal freedom, for, having defined one's self-worth by what one does, be it personal, social, or

occupational, he or she will find it next to impossible to give that up and do something else.
7. Can easily become hopeless about the future since, once having fallen into the trap of thinking his or her Self to be a worthless failure, he or she will easily conclude that such a worthless person could never succeed in the future.
8. Will likely fall into an exhausting, never-ending quest to prove his or her worth, for, once one challenge ends, whether that be a success or a failure, another will inevitably appear. He or she will not only find anxiety and/or depression a staple of life, but will exhaust oneself on this never-ending treadmill.
9. Can become vulnerable to bigotry toward others in that, having endorsed the twin perversions of self-identity and self-esteem, he or she may devilry other groups of people by virtue of some arbitrary trait a person possesses, say the color of one's skin, religion, or any number of behaviors or traits.
10. Will, having already damned oneself for some botched Do or substandard Have, likely damn himself or herself for being so weak as to become depressed, thereby creating secondary emotional disturbance on top of the original one.

Clearly the cost of endorsing the concept of self-esteem can be devastating. Facing this, the challenge to REBT is to detach the patient from this concept. To do this, the therapist leads the patient to skeptically dispute the belief, "I am worthless/a failure/not good enough," through two penetrating questions: (1) Is this belief true or valid? (2) Why not?

So, what are the answers to these two questions? Is there validity to the concept of self-esteem? Is there ever any logic to defining or esteeming one's self as all good (high self-esteem) or all bad (low self-esteem)? The answer to both is a resounding "No." Here are the main arguments against truth or the validity of the concept of self-esteem:

- As discussed earlier, it is not possible to define a person by any one act, role, or personal characteristic. As the philosopher John Locke (1632–1704) noted in the seventeenth century, the real essence of an object, in this case an individual human being, is beyond the power of sensory descriptions and thus cannot be defined by such characterizations as "man" or "university professor." There is indeed a self that exists, but this self is not equal to or defined by any of its observable acts or characteristics.
- The act of esteeming a person's Self or Being by some selected Do or Have is both arbitrary and capricious. You may, for example, determine to esteem your Self as worthy or unworthy based on gaining the approval of others. Others may base it on their IQ. Still others may select their financial success, their looks, or any one of a multitude of other variables to give themselves worth. But who has the authoritative power to objectively determine that this, that, or another factor is the ticket to human worth? Such a decision rests on an arbitrary choice, chosen at the whim of the individual's value system, and without any logical or empirical merit.
- Esteeming a person as all good or all bad based on a few acts or traits is an illogical overgeneralization, for these acts or traits exist in a sea of thousands of others. Certain of these acts or traits may be of greater value to the person or to society at large than others, but a person is hardly equal to these few acts or traits and can hardly be rated in total as all good or all bad by only these few. "I am all good because I did this one good deed" makes no logical sense, nor does "I am all bad because I did this one bad deed."
- To esteem a person as all good or all bad would require an impossible mathematical calculation. It would require a person to first have to remember and record each act ever performed throughout life, all the while sorting them into positive and negative categories. Then one would have to assign special weights to each of these positive and negative

actions. Thus, molesting a child would logically be given a substantially more negative weight than the positive weight given to paying one's mortgage on time. Obviously, no such weighting system exists. The mathematical absurdity of this continues in that one would then have to invent some formula onto which to plug in the raw number to come up with a figure, say eighty-nine. Finally, there would have to be a cut-off so that one could herd out the bad people (those with no worth and thus low self-esteem) from the good (those with worth and thus high self-esteem). Like at school, should seventy percent be the cut-off, whereby seventy and above puts the person in the good group, and sixty-nine and below assigns the person to the worthless ones? Doesn't all this sound impossible, if not absurd?

- A person is not a static object that exists only at a particular time and a particular location. Rather, he or she is an ever-changing process, one that adds, eliminates, and alters what one does and what one has on a day-by-day, if not moment-by-moment, basis. How can such an ever-changing person be legitimately frozen in time such that this person becomes rated as all good or all bad over a lifetime? Likewise, how can such a judgment of one's worth, once done, stay static when the panoply of one's acts and traits change from one day to the next? The answer to both questions: it can't. Even if we could esteem a person as all good or all bad at a given moment, we'd have to repeat this rating over and over, almost second-by-second, as that person travels relentlessly to the end of life.

All of this is why I call self-esteem one of the worst concepts ever invented. But if we destroy a person's belief in self-esteem, with what do we replace it?

The answer is Unconditional Self-Acceptance (USA). With USA, a person stubbornly refuses to ever define or evaluate one's

Self. He or she just accepts one's Self as alive and human, without definition or esteeming, and works for happiness rather than the affirmation of one's existence. He or she adheres to the principles: (1) I exist; (2) I am too complex and multifaceted to be defined by a singular label and/or an up-or-down report card; (3) while I exist, I will stubbornly refuse to rate, judge, or esteem my whole Self as either good or bad; (4) with happiness as my goal, I will rate, judge, and esteem my various performances and traits for they have relevance to the well-being and happiness of myself and others.

The route from self-esteem to self-acceptance can be long and hard. Why? Because virtually everything in our society explicitly or tacitly endorses the concepts of self and self-esteem. It takes long, hard, devoted effort to realize this transformation. But, for those I've treated who've done it, they've found happiness and peace of mind, along with the boldness to pursue cherished goals without fear. Isn't this what we would want for all our patients—and for ourselves?

Reference

Grieger, R., and Boyd, J. (1980). *Rational-Emotive Therapy: A Skills-Based Approach*. New York: Van Nostrand.

6

UNCONDITIONAL PERSONAL RESPONSIBILITY

The root source of extraordinary performance and results

It is not the critic who counts, nor the man who points out how the strong man stumbles. The credit belongs to the man who is actually in an arena, whose face is marred by dust and sweat and blood; who strives valiantly; who errs, who comes up short again and again; but who actually strives to do the deeds; who knows great enthusiasm, the great devotion; who spends himself in a worthy cause; who at the best in the end knows the triumph of high achievement; and who at the worst, if he fails, at least fails while daring greatly, so that his place shall never be with those cold and timid souls who neither know victory nor defeat.[1]

– *Theodore Roosevelt*

This powerful statement by President Roosevelt raises a provocative question: what does it take for a person to relentlessly do what is necessary, whatever that may be, despite obstacles and setbacks, to produce valued, intended results? Whenever I read it, it makes me think of the day I discovered *est*, the Erhard Sensitivity Training. Touted by friends as mind-blowing, it promised a profound personal transformation through the answering of two questions: (1) What is the *nature of being* for human beings? (2) What is the *possibility of being* for human beings? To say that these questions stimulated my curiosity would be an understatement.

So there I sat, theater-style, along with hundreds of other participants, over two consecutive weekends, in a downtown Washington D.C. hotel ballroom. Ceiling-to-floor curtains blocked the outside world from penetrating the room. Strict rules prohibited us from talking except when recognized by the trainer. We could not leave the room except at designated breaks or get out of our seats unless participating in some exercise. I figured that Werner Erhard designed all this to force we participants to look inward at ourselves.

The drama started immediately. Bespectacled, middle-aged Kevin, dressed in gray slacks, a starched white dress shirt, and a navy blue double-breasted blazer, stood up and, in a crisp baritone voice, asked the trainer to provide him a receipt for his tuition.

The trainer, Brian, also smartly dressed in black slacks, a dark green crewneck sweater, and a blue-collared shirt, walked slowly from behind his podium to look Kevin directly in the eye. He simply said, "No, I won't do that."

Kevin stood there, looking astonished, his mouth open. Brian held his gaze and waited in silence for him to respond. The room became funereal quiet. All eyes fixed on the two protagonists who looked like gunfighters waiting for the other to slap leather.

Kevin broke first. In an almost pleading voice, he said, "But I need the receipt for my income taxes."

Holding his gaze, Brian said, "This isn't about your income taxes, Kevin; it's about you."

Kevin stood silent for a few seconds, then, half defiant and half defeated, said, "But I have a right to it, I paid my money."

"Kevin, what's your real agenda here?"

Kevin's face flushed deep red. The room couldn't have been more silent. Brian continued to stare into Kevin's eyes, then said, "What I'm driving at, Kevin, is that you're a machine, built to mindlessly act out the pattern your cogs and wheels dictate. The sad thing is that you don't know it, what it's about, how it impacts your life." He then led Kevin through a conversation that gradually revealed how Kevin compulsively sought to maintain strict control over his environment in order to feel safe in his world.

He might be an est trainer on weekends, I thought, *but he must be one hell of a psychotherapist in real life.*

Throughout the rest of that day, Brian held one come-to-Jesus conversation after another with people who were hell-bent on making excuses for, blaming others for, or whining about their life's difficulties. There was the forty-something auto mechanic on the brink of a marital split-up who insisted he was the victim of his malnourishing and malevolent wife. There was the gray-haired grandmother who resented her family for their concerns about her drinking and insisted that, if they would only stop nagging her, she'd stop drinking. Then there was the twenty-two-year-old college drop-out who attributed his lack of motivation to his not as yet having found his true calling.

I watched this *est* trainer expose the rationalizations and excuses of each person he encountered. I saw him illuminate the patterned responses that stemmed from what he called their mind traps, cognitive programs, and repressed memories of traumatic incidents. I saw some accept the feedback, others fight against it, but all understand it. To each he delivered the same message: "You're a machine."

My turn to face my own machinery came on the third day of training. I returned from lunch to find the ballroom rearranged into five rows extending over the entire width of the room. In front stood a similarly wide wooden platform that rose some three feet above the floor, just deep enough for people to stand next to each other without falling off. Once we had settled into our seats, with me in the back row, Brian instructed those in the front row to walk to their right, file onto the platform, and stand facing the audience. The only instruction he gave was for both those "on-stage" and those in the audience to make eye contact with each other.

Some on the platform stood still, staring steadily into the eyes of the audience. Others gasped and fidgeted, breaking eye contact. A few covered their faces with their hands and wept. One or two actually fainted, caught by assistants standing behind the platform who gently laid them on the carpet while the exercise continued.

Watching this, my heart pounded, my chest filled with anxiety, my eyes darted around the room to locate exit signs. *Oh my God, I'll have to go through that too!*

After what seemed like an eternity, Brian then instructed row one to file off the platform and told us in row five that it was our turn. The slight relief I felt in knowing that my ordeal would soon be over did little to quell the fear that blocked rational thought. If I had been able to focus on the machinery of my mind, I would've seen that it was grinding out the thought, *Their judgment will crush me.*

Then, miracle of miracles, as I walked to the platform, I glanced sideways to the audience and saw people with scared looks in their own eyes. The thought passed through my mind, as precise as a whistle, as penetrating as an ice pick: *These people are just like me. They can't harm me. I'm safe.* Calm filled me. I felt at ease. Secure. Confident. I then used my time on-stage to lock onto the eyes of first one, then another, then another of those in the audience, never breaking eye contact until they did.

Gradually, over the course of these three days, I got the message, which is that we humans do not really control our lives. Rather, our present behaviors are no more than automatic, patterned responses based on deeply engrained beliefs, largely unconscious, programmed into us through our experiences, the result being that we mindlessly create a future that inevitably looks like our past. The human mind is a machine and, to the extent that we identify ourselves with our minds, we are ourselves machines. That is the *nature of being* for human beings. Sounded like REBT to me.

That night, pushing midnight, I laid in my hotel room bed, the only sound distant car horns, the only light the whitish glow of the electric clock-radio on the night table. I felt affirmed by *est*'s parallel to the theory of REBT. I fell asleep, peaceful, eager for the next day's grand finale, in which "the *possibility of being* for human beings" promised to be revealed.

People congregated for the last day of the training dressed as they had for the previous three—in slacks and jeans, sweaters and sport coats. But somehow they looked different. There was a bounce in their steps, smiles on their faces, a glint in their eyes. They looked as though they were gathered to celebrate the Beatles first reunion concert, to receive their coveted college diploma, to welcome the Messiah's holy word.

At exactly nine o'clock, Brian stepped to the podium, unexpectedly dressed in a dark blue suit, a blue Oxford dress shirt, and a blue and white striped tie. He slowly surveyed the room, left to right, scanning the participants as if he were seeing something known only to him. Then he asked, "So, what is the *possibility of being* for human beings?"

We sat silent, all eyes on him, waiting.

With an expression that showed no empathy or warmth, he thundered, "The answer is, there is no possibility whatsoever. Your mind is a machine, already programmed by your prefabricated belief systems, endlessly doing what it's built to do. Worse, you identify yourself with your mind such that you are a machine as well. As such, you will live endlessly at the mercy of the machine that is you. There is no help for you, no hope!"

If he wanted to get my attention, he got it. I stared, shocked, as if he had just told me that my beloved had betrayed me. *Are you kidding me?* I thought.

Brian again swept the room, this time in the opposite direction than before. Then he threw us a lifeline. "But, don't despair," he said. "There's a way out."

"Thank God," someone yelled from the back of the room. "Tell us before we blow our brains out."

Everyone laughed, even Brian. "Don't do that," he said, "but what you've got to do is blow out your minds."

Meaning? I thought.

He went on. "You've got to get rid of the self that you've always thought you are. You have your mind, but you are not your mind. You have your desires and feelings, your positions and defenses, but you are not any of these things. Your self is nothing, an empty space. But, out of that nothingness can come your power to make yourself anything you want."

Right on! I thought, happy to be back on the familiar REBT ground.[2]

Then Brian took me into new territory, for which I'll forever be grateful. He asserted that the only possibility of being for human beings comes from the distinction between what he called *Being at Effect*, the paradigm of Conditional Personal Responsibility, and *Being at Cause*, or that of Unconditional Personal Responsibility.

He turned to the chalkboard behind him and wrote on its left side in big, bold letters, "BEING AT EFFECT." Again facing us, he said, "*Being at Effect* is a belief, paradigm, or life position that sounds like this:

> 'How I act, the choices I make, and the results I produce ultimately depend on the circumstances operating at any given moment. So, when I give my word, make a commitment, or determine to make some goal a reality, I fully intend on following through and producing that result. But, if some circumstance arises between the making of that promise and

the point of completion that makes it difficult or unpleasant to keep it—whether it be an inner circumstance, such as adverse feelings, loss of motivation, changing priorities, or outer circumstance, the weather, traffic, other people—that circumstance justifies not keeping my word, honoring the commitment, achieving that goal. My life is at the effect of circumstances such that, instead of running my life, the circumstances run me.'"

I sat there, silent, along with the hundreds of other participants. *Wow*, I thought, clearly recognizing in myself the paradigm he just articulated.

During the rest of the morning Brian illuminated the mind trap of *Being at Effect* through participants who shared their stories. Instead of acting to create the adventures he wanted in his life, Robert played it safe, at the effect of his fear of failing. Instead of purposely acting to create a happy marriage, Stephen acted at the effect of his anger toward what he termed his wife's "inner bitch." Instead of doing what was necessary to find a longed-for lover, Paula shied away from dating at the effect of her belief in her own unlovability. These three people and many others demonstrated how they all operated at the effect of their mental machinery.

I got it and couldn't wait for *Being at Cause*, what Brian promised us to be the breakthrough, the transformation he would serve up to us after lunch.

Once reassembled, Brian wrote on the right side of the board, BEING AT CAUSE, in big, bold letters, and said:

"With your self being nothing but the empty space of possibility, you are free to create your self as the self you want. Being at Cause starts with you declaring that who you are is not your mind, but your word, your commitments, your promises. Your sacred word, to you, out of your choice, becomes the center of who you are, not your thoughts, feelings, motivation, or any of those other things inside of you. In practical terms, with this as your self-definition, you simply make a promise or a commitment to produce some future results; then, outside of your mind, you freely do whatever is necessary to achieve those results, despite all those psychological circumstances that may bedevil you. With your word being the center of you, you act on your word, not your circumstances. Instead of living from the past, propelled by the motor of your pre-existing mind, you freely live into the future, pulled forward by your commitments. You live at cause, not at effect."

I got it. I saw immediately that what Brian had just communicated that day was true of me. I got it that I had heretofore lived the victim of a paradigm, *Being at Effect*, I didn't even know I held, but one that had all too frequently driven my life choices. And I saw the alternative choice, *Being at Cause*. I felt freed, light and airy, powerful. It blew my mind.

That evening I drove east on US 66, then south on VA 29, passing through Gainesville, Warrenton, Culpeper, Madison, Ruckersville, and finally into Charlottesville. Lost in thought about that day's experience, I barely noticed the twilight easing into darkness, the purplish outline of the distant Blue Ridge Mountains, the grazing horses and cattle, the roadside stores and filling stations.

Unlike the first three days, which had paralleled the ABCs of human nature that Albert Ellis preached, today rocked my REBT world. I knew and embraced the truth in the ABCs, but I knew I now had something important I needed to integrate into it—*Being at Cause*, the paradigm of Unconditional Personal Responsibility. But how? In what way? With what kinds of emotional problems?

I knew I had some serious thinking to do. I made a commitment to flesh it out, starting the very next day.

Reflection

I have now spent countless hours thinking, talking, and teaching about the Unconditional Personal Responsibility paradigm of *Being at Cause*. Here, below, is what I have concluded so far.

First, action reigns supreme. Without acting, nothing happens, nothing changes, no results are produced.

I illustrate this in workshops by holding a pencil in my open palm and giving the following instruction to a volunteer: "Try to take the pencil from my hand." Invariably this person snatches it, as if I intended to pull it away at the last moment.

Most of the time this rouses laughter from the audience before I ask them, "Did he follow my instructions?"

Most chorus a "yes." But usually some astute person will get it. "No," this person says, "he took the pencil, but you told him to try to take it, not take it."

"That's right. I told him to try, not take it." I then retrieve the pencil and, again palm up, I repeat my prior instruction, "Try to take the pencil from my hand."

This volunteer stands staring at me, a perplexed look on his face.

"Here, let me show you what trying looks like," I say. With the pencil in my left hand, I clench my right claw-like and, grimacing and grunting, poke and prod all around the pencil, seemingly not able to penetrate an imaginary barrier.

Turning to the audience, I then ask, "That's what trying looks like. So what happens with trying?"

Several answer in unison, "Nothing."

"That's right," I say, then hold my hand out palm-up once again to the volunteer. "Now, take the pencil from my hand."

Once he does, I tell the audience, "See, the only thing that produces a result is doing what's necessary to bring about that result. Caring won't. Hoping won't. Trying won't. Only acting, doing what's necessary, will get the job done."

As simple as this concept is, few get it, even fewer live by it.

Second, like the ABCs of REBT, virtually no one has ever heard of the distinction between the Conditional Personal Responsibility paradigm of *Being at Effect* and the Unconditional Personal Responsibility one of *Being at Cause*. Like with me at the *est* seminar, people need to be educated. To do so, I instruct each participant in the seminar to write down three promises they recently made that they did not fulfill. Next to each, they are instructed to note the reason or excuse they gave to themselves or to another person to explain away why they did not keep them.

Most people complete this assignment in short order. I then assemble them in three-person groups and challenge each group to bat one hundred percent in collectively figuring out how they could have kept their commitments despite the difficulties they encountered. Invariably they report success.

Then the fun begins. I say, "Kinda backed you people into a corner, didn't I? You made a commitment to produce a result, didn't follow through, but now just proved you could have kept it. So, here's my question: why didn't you keep your word and produce the results?"

Almost always the audience sits silent, staring at me. I wait.

Finally someone says, "It was difficult."

"Yeah, but not impossible," I say.

Then another says, "My priorities changed," to which I reply, "But you gave your word."

Yet another says, "A conflict arose."

"I get that," I say, "but you just figured out how you could've kept your promise anyway, didn't you?"

The discussion goes on in this vein for a while until I say, "So what I'm hearing you say is that the reason why you didn't follow through on keeping your word was that you live by the PITA principle."

"What's that?" someone asks.

"Simple. You didn't act, didn't produce the result you promised, because it was a **P**ain **I**n **T**he **A**ss. You sacrificed your committed results for the circumstance of convenience and comfort. Worse, you sacrificed your integrity. I wonder what effect operating by that equation has on your desired results in a month, a year, even a lifetime?"

As a grand finale, I then share with the workshop participants the essence of *Being at Cause*:

> I, and no one else, am the source or cause of whatever I do or don't do. In any situation, I always have a choice, and I am always the chooser of the choice I choose. I will therefore choose to do what is necessary to produce the results to which I am committed. No excuses. No rationalizations. No holds barred.

Now, there is a third thing I have concluded. In the domain of personal responsibility, one has two and only two choices: one, *Being at Effect*; two, *Being at Cause*. There is no middle ground. At any given moment, one will stand on the ground of one or the other, but never on both. Though we in REBT abhor all-or-none, black-or-white thinking, this is indeed a black-and-white distinction: a person can align behind either the paradigm of *Being at Cause* or *Being at Effect*; there is no middle ground.

A fourth point is truly mind-blowing. One cannot choose to not make the choice between these two paradigms. In every second of our lives, whether realized or not, we have to choose either to *Be at Effect* or to *Be at Cause*. Personal responsibility is a paradigm that is always in play all day every day. Starkly stated, one cannot choose to not choose between these two paradigms.

So, fifth, as a REBT practitioner, I have spent a career helping hundreds upon hundreds of patients identify, eliminate, and replace the irrational paradigms that devil their lives. These have typically included the paradigms of Perfectionistic Demandingness, Catastrophizing, Low Frustration Tolerance, and Self-Rating.

I now appreciate the power of the Conditional Personal Responsibility paradigm of *Being at Effect* to also wreak havoc in a person's life. Just yesterday I addressed this with Charles. Several weeks ago, he presented himself as a man suffering from major depression. Fifty-seven years old with a shock of gray hair and the erect posture of the military man he used to be, he readily supplied me with all the necessary information to determine that the source of his depression was his errant self-damning.

Charles readily concurred with this feedback and agreed to do his daily psychotherapeutic assignments with a "Yes, sir." These included completing a work-sheet to identify, dispute, and replace his depression-causing irrational beliefs; following an activity schedule designed to get him out of his bedroom and back into a rewarding life; and engaging in recreational engagements with his wife.

Despite my best efforts, though, he didn't follow through, showing up for one appointment after another having made no effort to alter either his dysfunctional thoughts or his self-limiting behavior. Then I pulled out *est*.

Putting on my best conversational tone so as to conceal my intentions, I said, "You were with the military, weren't you, Charles?"

"Yes, sir, Marine Corps, thirty years."

"God, Corps, Country! Right?"

"You bet," he said, unsmiling, but with the first hint of vigor in his voice during that session.

"Never been in the military myself," I said, ready to spring my trap, "but my understanding is that the Marine code is all about duty, honor, and integrity, not just mindlessly following orders. Am I right?"

Charles hesitated a moment and eyed me as if calculating my direction. "I guess that pretty much hits the mark, Doc."

Looking at this gray-haired man, I sensed how badly he wanted to feel better and how much he pinned his hopes on me. *Here goes*, I thought.

I then explained to Charles the distinction between the two personal responsibility paradigms of *Being at Effect* and *Being at Cause*. After making sure he understood the difference, I asked, "When in the Marines Corps, which of these two codes did you live by?"

Without a second's pause, he said, "*Being at Cause*."

"I figured, Charles, but what about now—Cause or Effect?"

He startled as if a gunshot had exploded behind him and stared into my eyes, mute.

"Look, Charles," I said, "you'll never get out of this depression unless you do your psychotherapy work. And you'll never do your psychotherapy work so long as you act at the effect of your feelings. I know it's hard to put out effort and energy when depressed, but so what. Are you going to be at its mercy of your feelings or are you going to recapture the spirit of the Corps, honor your word, and do what's necessary out of the integrity of your commitment?"

That spurred Charles and me to review his between-session psychotherapy assignments. Then I asked for and he gave me his word, *at Cause*, as an officer and a gentleman, to follow through—no excuses accepted or tolerated.

I have found the personal responsibility paradigm of *Being at Cause* to be a good weapon in my REBT arsenal. The list of people who have benefited from the shift of *Being at Effect* to it grows. There is the twenty-one-year-old college sophomore who failed to complete three separate semesters, putting her two years behind her peers on the road to graduation. Recognizing her commitment to circumstances rather than her word opened the door to her sustained success. Then there is Fred, a recovering alcoholic with one relapse after another. Confronted with his self-indulgent commitment to pleasure rather than his word, he committed to his commitments and has now maintained sobriety for six months. And then there was Molly, depressed like Charles, who, upon aligning herself behind Unconditional Personal Responsibility and *at Cause*, fought her way free of this oppressive emotion.

Here, then, are some of the psychotherapeutic arenas in which a psychotherapist can make significant use of the Unconditional Personal Responsibility paradigm of *Being at Cause* to further a patient's mental health and well-being:

- Generating pleasurable and happy experiences;
- Acting to overcome depression;
- Refraining from addictive behaviors;
- Acting, not procrastinating;
- Building relationship trust and harmony;
- Time management;
- Acting assertively;
- Anti-anxiety risk-taking exercises;
- Sound parenting practices;
- The development of such character traits as integrity, honesty, industry, perseverance, and the like;
- Overcoming low frustration tolerance.

A final point. I have yet to work with a patient who did not harbor one or more of the four core irrational beliefs that cause most emotional disturbances. We psychotherapists would be wise to always check for and, when found, help our patients eradicate and replace them. Nevertheless, *Being at Cause* is such a powerful paradigm to produce valued results that I recommend never failing to inquire about its presence or absence and, if needed, earmark its attention in the psychotherapeutic game plan.

Notes

1 This is an excerpt from a speech titled, "Citizenship in a Republic," delivered at The Sorbonne in Paris, France, on April 23, 1910.
2 See Chapter 5, Destroy Self-Esteem.

7

PSYCHOLOGICAL FREEDOM

From misery, indecision,
compulsions, and addictions

What then is freedom?
The power to live
as one wishes.
— *Marcus Tullius Cicero*

What this inspirational quote communicates has provided inspiration for people throughout history. A thousand years before the birth of Christ, the Indian Upanishads captured the individual's sacred freedom to own one's personal land with the word *swaraj*. Five hundred years later, the Greek historian Thucydides told us about Pericles's funeral oration that glorified Athens as "the apostle of freedom." Fast forward to the seventeenth century A.D. when the English social philosopher John Locke, an inspiration for the American Revolution of 1776, argued that the sole purpose of government is to preserve and enlarge individual freedom.

But what could be more important than what we might call psychological freedom? While we may be the beneficiaries of all the freedoms that democratic societies can provide, we can still be enslaved from within by alienation, indecision, emotional misery.

Indeed, antiquity's The Bhagavad Gita asserted that the truly free person has transcended cravings. Centuries later, G. W. F. Hegel asserted that people are free to the extent that they overcome their selfish desires. More recently, Mahatma Gandhi demonstrated that one can only find freedom by conquering fear.

To be sure, REBT avidly champions psychological freedom. Its explicit goals are to help people care but not overcare, to liberate them from their compulsions and addictions, to rid them of the various manifestations of emotional misery they seem so adept at creating. Yet, it implicitly strives to bring all this about so that people can freely pursue those goals that they determine will lead to a life filled with happiness and productivity. It seeks no particular outcome for its patients, but strives to help them pursue their own cherished goals derived through a rational exploration of what's in their long-range best interests.

A healthy dose of psychological freedom was just what Kevin needed. A third-year mathematics major at the University of Virginia, he looked to be the All-American boy. He had the strapping body of a Texas football halfback, the blond good looks of a California surfer, the innocent face of an Indiana farm boy. Not just another pretty face, he carried close to a 4.0 GPA and played saxophone in a professional jazz quartet that lent him out for weekend gigs with local rock 'n' roll bands. He reminded me of the many young men I'd known when I was his age growing up in the Midwest—innocent, goodhearted, without guile—who would one day mature into a confident, successful adult.

Yet what Kevin wrote on his intake sheet stated otherwise. Under "Major Problems For Which You Want Help," he had printed in such tiny, constricted letters that I had to almost squint to read them, "Fragile sense of self-worth—constant feelings of anxiety and fear."

How could that be? I wondered, then asked him to flesh out some of the specifics about this self-description.

Kevin started by telling me about meeting an attractive young lady, Laura, on the ski slopes the weekend before. He described how anxious he felt the whole time he was with her, being practically tongue-tied at times, worrying about what his next move should be, whether she liked him or not. "Thank God we could escape into skiing instead of me just standing there mumbling like a fool."

"Wow, what an emotional ordeal you went through," I said, remembering feeling some of the same self-doubts with young ladies when I was his age.

"Well, I better buck-up quick," he said, "'cause we're scheduled to go on a hike together this coming Sunday afternoon."

"But that's too superficial, Kevin," I said. "The challenge for you is not to buck-up, but to free yourself of your anxiety so you can relax with her, be yourself, have some fun."

"Yeah, right, and do that by Sunday," he said, with a dash of sarcasm and a pinch of desperation. "How do I do that?"

"By first recognizing that the possibility of your goofing with Laura didn't throw you into panic. It was how you framed it, what you told yourself, your self-talk when you were right there with her. Think back. What was it?"

He paused, then said, "What if she doesn't like me," scrunching his face, as if he were re-experiencing the same pain he felt last weekend right there in my office.

"Meaning that to fail with her would be horrible," I said, "that you must succeed with her at all costs, that you would magically turn into a worthless nothing if she didn't like you?"

"Yep, exactly."

"Right," I said, "and that type of thinking is just what you've got to get out of your head, because it's what causes you to be anxious. Notice, though, the goal we're after is not getting Laura to like you, but to free you of your anxiety so that you can give it your best shot with her and also enjoy yourself in the process. Right?"

"Right."

"But before we do that, how about we first see how this kind of irrational thinking plays out in other areas of your life?"

Kevin then proceeded to describe how anxious he gets when he hangs out with guys with whom he isn't familiar, retreating within himself so as "not to show too much and be rejected." He shared the anxieties he experiences before every exam, fearing he might get less than an A and thus fail to be admitted into Massachusetts Institute of Technology. More exotic, he told me about how uptight he gets when playing the saxophone in public, not just when he sits in with a rock-and-roll band, but when he plays in a jazz quartet as well. He gets so nervous, he shared, that he's unable to let his improvisational creativity fly.

For each of these situations, we tracked down the same irrational thinking: "I *must* do exceptionally well and look absolutely sterling;" "It would be *horrible of me* to ever perform sub-par and be seen as less than glorious;" "To fail to do perfectly well would make me *a failure.*"

"See how it's the same with all these situations as it was with Laura, Kevin." I summed up: "Now, our job is to free you from these irrational thoughts so you can relax and enjoy life."

Kevin made quick strides in his REBT by both challenging his irrational beliefs and acting against them. In short order he went to a bar where he chatted with people of both genders without feeling anxiety. He was able to study for an important physics exam anxiety-free. He even joined a salsa dance club in order to meet women without feeling any discomfort.

Just a few days before I wrote this, Kevin walked into my office, his saxophone hanging from a strap slung over his shoulder. A big grin split his face as he plopped onto the couch.

"Am I getting a concert today?" I asked.

"You got it," he said, then stood up, brought the reed to his lips, and did a perfect imitation of the late Clarence Clemons rocking out behind Bruce Springsteen.

I sat enthralled, tapping my feet in time with the music.

Once finished, he let the saxophone hang from its strap, smiled, and said, "So, what'd you hear?"

"Great music," I said.

"Yeah, thanks," he said, "but, more than that?"

"What?"

"You just heard the sound of me being free to be myself. I can now improvise as I want rather than be enslaved by the ghost of Charlie Parker."

Then there was Toni and Don, a couple emotionally overwrought, confused, at the end of their rope. They wanted me to help them find a practical solution to their dilemma, rather than the freedom to find it for themselves.

"What brings you two?" I asked after they settled next to each other on the couch across from me.

Don darted his eyes toward Toni who immediately dropped her chin to chest. "I'll let Toni go first," he said.

With that, Toni shielded her eyes with her hand and began to sob. Don put his arm around her shoulders, pulled her to him, and enclosed her with his other arm. "This is the way she's been for close to a month now," he said, looking pleadingly at me while continuing to embrace her.

"It's okay, Toni," I said. "Take your time and when you're ready you can tell me about the problem."

I studied them while she gathered herself. Don looked to be in his mid-thirties, of medium height. He wore rumpled blue work pants, an oil-stained long-sleeved white shirt with the name of the auto repair company where he worked sewn to his breast pocket. Also in her thirties, full-figured but not overweight, Toni wore a black sweater, a red and black paisley skirt, and black socks that rose to just below her knees. Her dark brown hair hung to her shoulders, but looked unwashed and rumpled. She looked like a secretary, which she was.

Once calmed, she tidied the hem of her skirt, and, with tightened lips, nodded, ready to talk. "I don't know what to do, I just don't know anymore. I'm just super depressed,"

"What are you depressed about, Toni?" I asked.

Between sobs, she told me that she had failed to follow through on three New Year's resolutions she set for herself—to work out at the gym, to take a dance class, to re-start her watercolor painting.

"Ah," I said, "so you've convinced yourself that you are therefore a totally worthless person and you carry that conviction around in your head as if it were God's gospel truth. Is that right?"

"That thought dominates my thinking," she said softly. She sighed and sat silent for a moment, then said, "I am worthless. I don't contribute anything to society at all. I'm disconnected from my own passions. I do nothing right."

Don took her hand and looked at me. "Doc," he said, "there's more than what she just told you."

"And what's that?" I said, eager to hear the rest of the story.

Don went on to explain that they had a wedding planned in two months and she feels panicked about what to do. He glanced at Toni, urging her to open up.

She took a long, deep breath, slowly exhaled, and then said, "One day, during the break, I started doubting whether or not I loved Don. I had been madly in love with him, but then I started not feeling it as strongly. Sometimes I just feel nothing. Do I really love him? Do we do enough that makes us happy? Are we as good as other couples? I get physically ill worrying if I should marry him."

REBT psychotherapists pay much less attention to making a formal diagnosis of mental illness than they do to ferreting out the ABCs of the patient's disturbance. Nevertheless, the more I listened to Toni, the more I entertained the idea that she suffered from a Borderline Personality Disorder. One of its primary features is a very fragile sense of self-identity and a vulnerable sense of self-worth. Such patients readily damn themselves whenever they fail at something or are rejected. Another feature of a Borderline Personality Disorder is what is called splitting. In splitting, the patient judges people in black-and-white terms—the other person is either adored as the greatest human to ever walk the face of the earth or abhorred as the lowest creature who ever lived. I wondered if she now thought that way about Don or even the relationship itself.

While I pondered all this, Toni interjected, "I just don't know whether the relationship is making me depressed or my depression is affecting how I feel about Don? I'm so confused that I sometimes want to kill myself. What do you think I should do, Dr. Grieger?"

Don then chimed in, "I'm not putting pressure on her, but, Doc, should we get married or not? We've got the date set, the venue reserved, the minister coming, the invitations sent out, and the cake ordered ..."

The desperate stare each of them gave me bore to my heart. This then was the challenge I faced: sitting before me was a deeply disturbed woman with a significant decision on her hands, the resolution of which would not only have a great impact on her future, but that of her fiancé as well. She was, however, a person without the psychological freedom to make a decision, any decision, much less one made rationally. And she, as well as Don, wanted me to supply her with the answer as to what to do.

Knowing that I had to disappoint each of them, I first said to Toni: "Look, I can't tell you how sorry I feel for what you're experiencing—the emotional pain, the indecision, everything. But I'm afraid you're putting the horse before the cart. You see, you have two problems here, one practical and one psychological.

The practical one is whether or not to marry Don; the psychological one is your deep depression, caused by your errant self-damning. The mistake you're making is that you want to solve your psychological problem by fixing your practical problem, whereas the only sensible thing to do is to first fix your psychological problem in order to free yourself to make the right decision that would fix your practical one. Do you follow me?"

Toni looked at me for what seemed like minutes. Finally she said, "So, you're telling me that I've got to free myself of my emotional disturbance before I can be trusted to make a sound decision about marrying Don?"

"Yes," I said, leaning forward, holding her gaze. "With you being so emotionally overwrought and with such self-damning going on inside you, I don't see how you can trust yourself to make the right decision. And, frankly, it's more than just about this one decision we're talking about, for with your self-worth so connected to everything you do, you'll be alternatively anxious and depressed the whole of your life unless you first get yourself fixed. Do you understand?"

"I think I do," she said, with what I thought to be a hint of relief in her eyes.

"And, Don," I said, "you would also be wise to think along these same lines, for this lovely lady sitting next to you is only going to be good for herself, and frankly good for you as a wife, if she makes positive strides with regard to her emotional problems. If she does, then she'll be free to know what she wants: if it's you, she'll be free to be a good partner; if not, your life will be a living hell, along with hers."

"Can she be fixed, Doc?"

"Yes, if she works long and hard, but not likely in the next eight weeks."

"What about the wedding then?"

"What do you think?"

"I guess it's best we postpone it and see what happens with her therapy."

"What do you say, Toni?" I asked.

"Can we do that without Don hating me?"

"Don?" I said.

"I love you and want you to be happy," he said, "with or without me."

"The question is, Toni, can you not hate yourself?" I asked.

"I'll try," she said.

"Well, that's what your psychotherapy will be all about," I said, "first getting rid of your self-hatred so that you are then free to make the decisions in your life that are right for you. That's what I'm here to help you do, if you'd like."

And that's what she did. As I write this, Toni and I continue to meet twice a week to avidly work on re-indoctrinating her irrational self-damning beliefs. Her progress is slow, but steady. Don continues to support her. We shall see the outcome in due time.

As a last example of the importance of psychological freedom, consider Amber, a woman of average height with a slender body, who came to her first session wearing a baggy pair of slacks and sweater that seemed a size too big for her. Her brownish blond hair, disheveled, with strands loose at each temple, topped a long face devoid of color and seemingly without muscle tone. She neither smiled nor made eye contact with me on her way to the couch.

Once seated, she handed me a photograph and said, "This is what I want back—my boys. Please help me figure out how to do that."

I studied the picture and couldn't help but notice how different she looked in the picture compared to the person sitting before me, tanned and healthy, with a full-mouthed smile and merriment in her eyes. To her left sat her two boys, early teenagers, handsome, similarly tanned. The older boy, sitting next to

Amber, looked straight into the camera and held a tightlipped smile of bemusement. The younger one leaned his head on his brother's shoulder and held his eyes impishly wide open.

"You three look so happy there, Amber," I said. "What happened?"

Here's the story she told. In 2007, both of her parents died within six months of each other. To help quell her heart-wrenching grief, she began to drink alcohol for the first time. As it provided only temporary relief, she gradually increased her drinking frequency to daily and her consumption to between six and twelve glasses of wine per day. During the past eighteen months, she began to experience detox tremors if she didn't consume alcohol in the morning. As her drinking increased, her self-care worsened, along with her marital relationship and her capacity to care for her children.

By 2016, things had deteriorated to the breaking point. In January, Amber's husband had her arrested after she drove her children to their sporting events while she was intoxicated. Again in June, he had her detained for endangering her children and a judge issued a protective order against her. When she violated this order a month later, the judge sentenced her to twenty days in jail, to be followed by a minimum of forty-five days of residential treatment. Admitted in early August, she was treated for her Severe Alcohol Abuse Disorder with a combination of twelve-step and cognitive-behavioral strategies. She was also medicated for her Major Depressive Disorder and Dependent Personality Disorder with a cocktail of Prozac, Effexor, and Gabapentin.

"Will you help me?" she asks.

"I will," I said, "by doing my best to help free you from both your depression and alcoholism." I then asked, "What did you learn during those forty-five days?"

"That I'm an alcoholic. That I'll totally ruin my life if I ever drink again. That I'm always in danger of drinking if I'm not alert."

"Wow," I said, "I'm impressed. You sure have gotten way past denial. That's an exceptionally important first step, as you know. But do you know what triggers your drinking?"

"Yes," she said, without missing a beat. "I get triggered when I'm upset—with guilt, depression, resentment, self-pity. The first thing I think about at these times is to jump into the bottle."

While she talked, I put the letter "A" on the left side of the whiteboard beside me; above it I put the words "Activating Event," and under it the words "Emotional Pain." And on the right side I put the letter "C" with the word "Consequence" above it. Then I put the words "Choose to Drink" under it. Between these two letters I wrote a large "B" with the word "Beliefs" above it (see Figure 7.1).

"Let me explain what I've just diagramed," I said. "Your trigger is the A and drinking is the C. But it's not the emotional pain per se at A that causes you to choose to drink at C. Millions of people go through emotional pain and don't drink. It's the way you think at B, your beliefs about the pain, that compels you to drink. When you're emotionally upset, Amber, what goes through your mind that drives you to drink?"

I noticed as I talked that Amber had scooted up to the front of the couch, leaned forward, and, with her chin leaning on her fists, stared at the whiteboard with the intensity of Einstein contemplating relativity. Finally, she said, "I can't stand to feel this way."

"That's right," I said, "and ...?"

"... I've got to get rid of my pain."

"... and ...?"

Figure 7.1 Amber's road to alcohol

"... and I've got to drink to feel better."

I clapped my palms together and pulled them apart, palms up, like a blackjack dealer does when turning the table over to his replacement. "Voilà," I said, "that's the key to your compulsion to drink—your automatic and deep-seated belief that your emotional pain is so horribly unbearable that you must find immediate relief. If you get rid of that nutty thinking, you will no longer feel compelled to drink. You'll be free to choose not to."

Still staring at the whiteboard, her face now scrunched instead of studious, she asked, "But what should I think?"

"How about," I said, "'I don't like feeling upset, sometimes even hate it, but I'm not a two-year-old and I can stand it. Emotional pain won't shatter me into a million pieces. Now, what can I do that's constructive to help myself feel better?' How does that sound to you?"

A smile blossomed on her face; it wasn't quite the same as the picture she showed me of her boys and her when she first walked into my office, but in the same ballpark. "In my in-patient sessions, they did teach me to use self-pleasing techniques when upset, like listening to music, contacting a friend for support, doing exercise."

"There you go!" I said. "Those are great strategies. I encourage you to use them, anything to not drink. But I'm suggesting that you do something more elegant, something that is actually more long-lasting than those immediate feel-good tactics. You can use the same ABC model I just diagramed to uncover and correct the actual cause of your emotional pain so that, with some work, you can eliminate it in a deep and healthy way."

"Really?"

"Really! Let me show you by considering something that you think causes you pain. Can you think of something?"

"Sure, I feel guilty and ashamed about my alcoholism."

"Okay," I said, writing on the whiteboard as I talked, "your Activating Event, the A, is your alcoholism, and your Emotional

Consequence, your C, is your guilt and shame. What do you think about or tell yourself at B to cause yourself to feel this way?"

"That's easy, that I'm a lowlife, worthless person—a total failure."

"There you have it, Amber. Anybody would make herself feel guilt-ridden thinking that way. That kind of thinking can be fixed too, with hard work. Make sense?"

"I think so," she said, drawing out the words, looking perplexed.

"Here, let me pull it all together for you."

I then drew the two-phase ABC sequence on the whiteboard that illustrated the complete picture of her compulsion to drink (see Figure 7.2). In Phase One, her irrational self-damning at B caused her emotional pain. In Phase Two, her catastrophizing about experiencing the pain led her to drink to relieve the pain.

Once I made sure Amber understood all this, I told her that my job was to help her correct the underlying cause of her alcoholism. But I also told her that I couldn't do it for her. She'd have to do the work to fix herself. "Will you commit to doing that?" I asked.

"Will it help me get back my boys?"

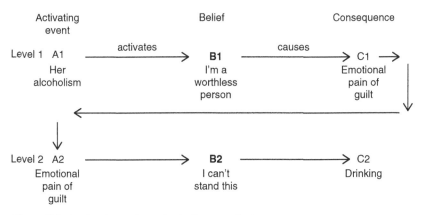

Figure 7.2 Amber's road to alcohol expanded

"Probably," I said. "If you follow the plan of action the court's demanded, including your therapy, and maintain your sobriety, I do think there's a good chance they'll reunite you with your children. But look, Amber, my job is not to help you get your kids back. Rather, it's to help you free yourself of your compulsive drinking so you can make good choices in your life. Getting your kids back will follow naturally from freeing yourself from irrational thinking, emotional contamination, and compulsive drinking. Do you understand that?"

"Yes," she said.

"Okay," I said, "so let's schedule an appointment and get right to work."

Reflection

St. Augustine wisely tells us that "The will is free when it is not the slave of vice, passion, and sin." REBT heartily endorses this assertion, but with the secular substitution of the words "irrational thinking" for "vice," "unhealthy emotional overreactions" for "passion," and "compulsions" for "sin."

When people think irrationally, they create the kinds of poisonous emotions that can easily overwhelm reason, good judgment, and the ability to inhibit immediate action in favor of long-range goals. Each of the three people in this chapter—Kevin, Toni, Amber—found themselves enslaved. Once freed from their poisonous beliefs, they were free to be happy, to take control of their lives, to make the kind of choices that would help them achieve their goals.

Through his REBT, Kevin is working to free himself from the misery of anxiety, which will allow him to pursue his academic, social, and musical goals, while at the same time allowing him to be peaceful and happy in the process. For Toni, the goal is for her to be free of the depression generated by self-damning, which poisons her ability to know and act on what she wants in her life. Amber's freedom must come in layers—first, freedom to gracefully tolerate emotional discomfort, then freedom from enslavement to alcohol, and, finally, freedom from depression.

For these three people, plus all the others I have and will treat through my clinical practice, I want nothing less for them than to walk from my office after our last appointment singing:

"Free at last! Free at last!
Thank God almighty,
I am free at last!"

8

THE PURSUIT OF ELEGANCE
Beyond feeling better to getting better

*There is no greater joy
nor greater reward
than to make a fundamental
difference in someone's life.*
— Sister Mary Rose McGeady

The sentiment Sister McGeady expresses is a treasure. In my opinion, her most important word is "fundamental," as in profound, significant, central, for that's what we psychotherapists strive for with all our patients, a fundamental change, like with forty-seven-year-old Shelly.

Slightly overweight, pale complexioned, and outfitted in a gray sweatsuit, she circled a wide berth around me as she made her way to my office couch. Averting my eyes, she scrunched herself deep into its corner as if she wanted to disappear. *This'll be a challenge*, I thought.

Quite the contrary. Once I asked her to tell me about the "Depression and PTSD" she had written on her intake sheet, Shelly told a startling story. Four years previously, when consulting a hypnotherapist about her chronic depression, memories of a series of sexual molestations flooded her consciousness. The first was at the age of fourteen when she was raped by an uncle in the basement of her parents' house. Then, during her sophomore year in college, when twenty, her boyfriend acted upon her a number of vile and violent abuses, including forcibly shaving her pubic hair, strangling her during intercourse to the point of unconsciousness, and urinating on her while she showered. Remembering all this filled her with such terror that she barricaded herself inside her home from that day forward.

As Shelly told her story, her eyes filled with tears and her hands trembled. Then she began to sob, great chest-heaving sobs that made her talk in lurches and gasps. She punctuated her narrative with words like "unbearable," "horrific," and "unstandable."

I had the impulse to hold her hand, pat her arm, even drape my arm around her shoulders, anything to comfort her. Knowing that she might find this threatening, however, I settled for a feeble, "I'm sorry you went through all that."

Shelly took two tissues from the Kleenex box on the table next to her, dabbed her eyes, and released a long deep sigh. She glanced at me, looked to her lap, then murmured four statements, each separated by a long pause, which taken together exposed the depths of her despair:

"That changed my life forever."
"It destroyed who I was supposed to be."
"I'll never be the same again."
"I'll never get through this."

Shelly and I both sat still, silent, while I absorbed her words and she picked imagined lint from her sweatpants. Just then, a door slammed somewhere in the building. She bolted upright in her seat, grabbed the armrest as if she were on an airplane experiencing turbulence, and darted her eyes to the door behind me.

"It's okay," I said, "just a noisy neighbor down the hallway." Then, after a pause, I said, "Do you startle like this at home?"

THE PURSUIT OF ELEGANCE   125

"Yes, I'm constantly afraid of noises, car doors slamming, horns honking, people talking when they walk by. It's been getting worse. I even fear noises inside the house now."

"What goes through your mind when you hear these noises?"

"That somebody is going to break in and hurt me, that I'm not safe, that I'm in danger."

While I feel empathy for the adversities people experience and the anguish they suffer, I make a point to listen for any expressions of the irrational beliefs that drive their misery. And there they were, stark and naked, the ABCs of both Shelly's PTSD and depression (see Figure 8.1). In direct response to her molestations (at A1), she unwittingly endorsed two life-changing beliefs (B1) which she held to be unquestionably true: one, there existed danger everywhere and she was never safe from harm; and two, it would be too horrible to bear ever going through such trauma again. These beliefs, held as gospel truths, caused all her PTSD symptomology (at C1).

But it didn't end there for Shelly. Her own anxieties also served as a secondary Activating Event (an A2). In response to these, she imposed the conviction (at B2) that her life was hopeless and doomed, thereby causing her to experience the secondary emotional disturbance of depression (at C2).

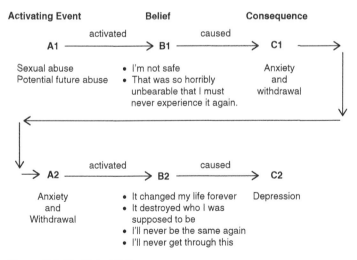

Figure 8.1 Shelly's ABCs

Once I understood all this, I drew Shelly's ABCs on my whiteboard and took her step-by-step through them, emphasizing the critical role her beliefs played in her disturbance. After making sure she understood all that, and validating that what I had written rang true to her, I gestured to the board and said, "Shelly, since you've brought this anxiety and depression on yourself by your own irrational thinking, you can get rid of it."

"Do you really think I can, Dr. Grieger?"

"I absolutely do," I said, perhaps a little louder than necessary, trying to sound as affirmative as possible. "Anything learned can be relearned. But it'll take a lot of hard work on your part—and courage."

She suddenly jerked her head back and looked at me from the corners of her eyes. "Courage?" she said, as if I had just asked her to walk barefoot over hot coals.

"Yes, courage," I said. "You've got to courageously assault your beliefs until you clearly see how unsound they are, but, just as important, you've also got to act against your fears."

She stared at me, her face drained of color. Putting her hand over her mouth, she whispered, "Oh, God."

Right there and then, I knew I had to act contrary to the typical REBT approach. Instead of immediately honing in on Shelly's most central evaluative belief as I normally would—that is, her conviction that another molestation would destroy her—I chose instead to tackle her perceptual distortion that she was in constant danger. It was not in fact realistic for her to believe she was in such peril, but, even if she were, she would still not have anxiety if she didn't catastrophize about it. I judged that she did not presently have the strength to defeat her catastrophizing without first feeling safe.

"It's okay, Shelly," I said to calm her. "We'll tackle this a little at a time, starting with the more concrete of your beliefs, 'I'm not safe,' and build a case against its truthfulness. Once you start believing it's not true, you'll find it so much easier to face people out there in the real world. Then we'll tackle the deeper of your irrational beliefs."

"But it is true; I'm not safe," she said without hesitation, ignoring the rest of my message. I read this as both an assertion of how deeply she believed it to be true and a plea not to be asked to test it.

"I know you believe it to be true," I said. "But, look, Shelly, just because you believe it, doesn't make it so. Let's together hold it up as a hypothesis and explore as to whether or not it's true. Let's let logic, reason, and empirical evidence tell us the truth, not your automatic habits of thinking."

Slowly, calmly, I then led Shelly through an intellectual exploration of the validity of the first of her core anxiety-producing beliefs: "I, Shelly, am not safe with anyone, anywhere, ever, and it's therefore correct for me to be so afraid that staying home is my best strategy." As expected, I had to take the lead, but felt gratified when, a few minutes into the process, she asked for paper and pencil so she could make notes of our reasoning.

Here then are the arguments we created to disprove this belief:

- Except for two individuals—her uncle some forty-three years previously, and her boyfriend in college, thirty-eight years ago—no other human being out of the hundreds she has encountered has ever abused her in any way, shape, or form. These two people are anomalies out of the thousands she has crossed paths with over the years.
- No one on the face of the earth holds the conscious intention to do her harm—absolutely no one.

- While all of us are potentially the victim of some random act of violence, she is just as safe as everyone else in the world. In fact, she is more safe than many, as compared, for example, to those in inner city crime zones or those in the strife-torn areas of the Middle East.

She laid her papers on her lap, looked at me, and released a sigh of fatigue.

"Tired?" I asked.

"Yes."

Leaning forward, I looked into her eyes and said, "We're almost done today, but, Shelly, listen, the forty-five or so minutes you spend with me is measly compared to the time you spend with yourself outside of this office. Your real therapy is out there, in your real life, re-indoctrinating the thinking that causes your anxiety, while I coach you in here on how to get yourself better. Okay?"

"Okay" she said, drawing out the word in a way that communicated, "Oh no, here it comes."

"What I urge you to do between now and our next appointment is something you'll find difficult, but something I know you can do. Each day, leave your house and go somewhere where there are people. It can be anywhere, even the relative safety of your front yard where people walk or drive by. I don't care who, where, or when; it makes no difference. Just do it. But here's the kicker: don't shy away, look at these people, and forcefully remind yourself that you are safe, consciously going over the three truths you wrote down. I have to be honest with you: your future happiness depends on it. Will you do it?"

She agreed and, after scheduling another appointment three days hence, we parted. I felt rung out. It was sad, heartbreaking, even tragic, to think of the years this poor person had lost to her misery and desolation. All I could do was wait and hope she summoned the courage to begin her healing process before we met again.

And she did, with trepidation and without much immediate success, but, dammit, she did it. I praised her for her effort, reassured her that it would eventually pay off, encouraged her to keep at it. Slowly, over the next two months, she expanded her range, from her front yard to the grocery store and the gym; her duration, from just a few minutes to an hour to hours at a time; and her boldness, from just glancing at people to looking them in the eye to actually smiling at and talking to them.

One day, gloomy and gray, Shelly walked in and brightened the room with her smile. "I've had no anxiety for a whole week," she said. "I think you've cured me, Dr. G."

Looking at this rejuvenated woman before me, at peace and cheerful for the first time in decades, I felt a rush of happiness. Yet I also felt a stab of regret, mixed with trepidation, because I knew I'd have to now push her once again out of her comfort zone if she was going to go beyond just feeling better to truly getting better.

"You have certainly come a long, long way, Shelly, and I'm impressed with how courageously you've acted." Then I quickly added so as not to back off, "But I'm afraid we've got more difficult work to do to really cure you."

She stared at me, her face still holding a smile, but one now frozen in place.

"Look, Shelly, you are indeed just as safe as anyone else is. But the truth is, no one is totally safe—no one! Both you or I could get killed in a car accident today. Both of us could be the victims of a terrorist attack tonight. Both of us could be assaulted by a lunatic tomorrow."

She suddenly turned ashen and cupped her mouth with both hands. "Oh God, Jesus, oh God," she whimpered. "Help me, Jesus, help me, oh God, please help me …"

"It's okay, Shelly," I said in as strong and reassuring a voice as I could muster. "This gets us to the core of your anxiety—your belief that, should you ever be molested again, it would be so horrible that you couldn't bear it."

With her hands still covering her mouth, she cried out without taking a breath, "But I couldn't bear it, I couldn't, I just couldn't."

"That's what you said when we first started disputing your belief that you weren't safe, don't you remember?" I said, unwilling to let her reinforce her catastrophic thinking unchallenged. "By looking hard at that belief, you proved to yourself that it wasn't true. And you can do that again with this one, that is, if you show the same courage as you did then."

"But it is true!"

"No, it's not, and I can prove it, if you'll let me. Okay?"

"Okay," she said, so soft I could barely hear her.

"Well, then," I said, "You did in fact bear it before. Therefore, God forbid, if it were ever to happen again, you could and would bear it once more."

"But I didn't."

"But you did. The very fact that you're sitting here today talking to me proves that you did indeed bear it. It didn't kill you then and it wouldn't now."

Shelly paused, slowly lowering her hands to her lap. *Good,* I thought, *I've got her away from her emotions and onto thinking about her thinking.*

"Well," she finally said, "I guess I did bear it—physically. But I didn't bear it emotionally. It ruined my life."

"But, Shelly, don't forget what the ABCs tell us—it was not what happened to you at A that caused you to experience your fear at C. It was your believing at B that it was horribly unbearable. Now, no one blames you for thinking that way. Who wouldn't? But, if you can own that you had a hand in creating your anxiety back then with your catastrophic thinking, and that you're keeping it alive today by still thinking that way, then we have a fighting chance to rid you of that thinking and your fear forever, no matter what may happen in the future."

"Do you really think I can?" she asked.

"I do," I said. "You did it once already, so there's no doubt that you can do it again. And I'll be alongside you every step of the way. I promise."

Together, then, Shelly and I listed as many reasons as we could to prove why the belief, "It would be so horribly unbearable to ever be again molested that it must never happen," was both untrue and invalid. As we did, I wrote them on a legal pad for her to use later, as follows:

- I am just as safe as everyone else on the face of this earth, as no one is out there with the intention of singling me out for harm.
- If it unfortunately were ever to happen again, I could and would survive and bear it—I did it once, and I could do so again.
- Should I ever be assaulted again, in any way, shape, or form, it would be limited to a very short period of time—once it's over, it's over, and I could again get on with my life.
- Even if I were to go through that again, the experience doesn't take away all the good things that are and continue to be part of my life—my family, my friends, my job, my health, my future.
- No matter what happens to me in the future, I will still be alive and human and have both the right and responsibility to fill my life with as much richness and happiness as I possibly can—and I will see to it that I do just that.

Once done, I tore the sheet from my legal pad and handed it to Shelly. "You know what you've got to do now, don't you?"

"I'm afraid I do," she said, smiling.

I smiled back, then said, "Yeah, you've got to continue to go out and be around people, reminding yourself that you're just as safe as everyone else. And you've also got to work, work, work to re-indoctrinate your thinking about not being able to bear it should the unlikely ever happen again."

"But how?"

"What you do, Shelly, is what I call 'The Six and the Five.' Six times a day—breakfast, mid-morning, lunch, mid-afternoon, supper, and sometime before bedtime—meditate for five minutes on exactly why it would not be unbearable. Be careful, though, to really think about the five points we came up with so that you can come to grasp and believe them to be true. We'll add more strategies to that later, but that's a good start."

Shelly promised to do her therapy each day until our next appointment. I reassured her she could contact me anytime, day or night, for support or coaching. She took her leave.

I sat at my desk and gathered myself before welcoming my next patient. I felt assailed with a conflux of emotions—relief that I had successfully led Shelly to the core of her anxiety, sorrow that she once again had to relive her trauma, resentment that such injustice had been acted upon her. Above all, I felt hope that this woman's life would now change dramatically—elegantly—for the better. I knew I'd do my part and was hopeful she'd do hers.

Reflection

Central to the practice of REBT is the distinction between elegant and inelegant change. In inelegant change the psychotherapist focuses on the fringes. He or she variously attempts to provide symptom relief at C, alter adverse circumstances at A, and/or correct perceptual distortion of reality at B.

While these types of interventions often help a person feel better, at least in the near term, they do not attack the core cause of the patient's mental health problems—their irrational beliefs. So, while experiencing temporary relief from suffering, the person remains vulnerable to flare-ups of symptoms when once again facing the same or similar life adversities. It is like treating the pneumonia sufferer with pain relievers, nasal decongestants, and cough suppressants, all helpful for comfort, but not effective in killing the bacteria in the person's lungs with antibiotics.

In elegant change, the REBT psychotherapist bypasses these relatively superficial strategies and works to track down, destroy, and replace the irrational beliefs that directly cause the patient's core emotional disturbance. He or she knows that symptom relief will naturally result from such change, that the patient will be a better problem-solver without the emotional contamination these irrational beliefs cause. And, if problem-solving is impossible, then the patient can gracefully lump the unwanted adversities without the contamination of painful overreactions.

I take great pains to provide elegant solutions to each of my patients, as exemplified by the five people below with whom I've counseled within the last weeks:

- Rather than reassuring Susan that her new boyfriend cared for her, or that she would find another beau if he didn't, I focused her on destroying the irrational beliefs that caused her anxiety and desperation—that this man must want her, that she must have a man in her life to be happy, that her value as a person derived from her being valued by him or some other man.
- Rather than working with anxiety-ridden Laurie to brainstorm strategies to help prevent her fifteen-year-old daughter from getting pregnant, I led her to challenge the conviction that an unwanted pregnancy would be so horrible that her daughter's life would be forever ruined.

- Rather than teaching Beverly and Ted sound communication skills to use when in conflict, I helped them rid the perfectionistic demands they each imposed on the other that stimulated the anger that blocked their ability to communicate effectively.
- Rather than reassuring twenty-two-year-old Samuel that his grade point average was sufficiently high to get into the graduate school of his choice, I helped him see that it was not necessary for him to do so to be a worthwhile person.
- Rather than comforting Sara with the prediction that she would soon be reunited with her children, I helped her tackle the belief that she needed to see her children in order to maintain her sobriety and that she was a horrible person because of her addiction.

In each of these cases, rather than working to alter their perception of gloom and doom, I had them assume the worst—for Susan that she might not find the love of her life, for Laurie that her daughter might get pregnant, for Samuel that he might not get into Harvard or Stanford. I then directed them to elegantly challenge the irrational beliefs that reality must match their desires, that it would be catastrophic and unbearable if it didn't, that they and their lives would be worthless under those circumstances. By doing so, they could not only cure the source of their emotional misery, but they could operate from the best of both worlds. They could work diligently to make what they wanted a reality and experience peace of mind—that is, live without anxiety, anger, or depression, whether they got what they wanted or not.

The REBT rule of thumb is to elegantly address the core irrational beliefs first and then, if still desired, clean up faulty perceptions, teach feel-good strategies, problem-solve the adversity. The concern is that, with inelegant symptom relief, the patient will feel so much better that he or she will prematurely terminate therapy without actually being cured.

That was my challenge with Shelly. While I knew that her elegant cure was her catastrophizing, I judged her too emotionally fragile to tolerate an assault in her current way of thinking at the beginning of her treatment. I figured that she would first have to find some relief from her fear, not to mention trust in me, a man after all. She would have to be willing and able to challenge the core belief that to be molested again would be too horrible to bear.

Thankfully, my strategy paid off. Shelly succeeded in inelegantly changing her perception of reality, from seeing herself as unsafe to seeing she was just as safe as everyone else. This perceptual shift not only brought her much-needed emotional relief, but, more importantly, it gave her the confidence she needed to take on the validity of her catastrophizing.

And that, I'm happy to report, is what she did. She now lives her life with no more fear than the average person and travels outside her house at will. I still meet with her weekly, but the focus now is on ridding her of her depression. With an elegant focus, I see no reason why she can't have as much success with this malady as she did with her PTSD anxiety.

9

MAKE WAR ON PERFECTIONISM
Be perfectly imperfect

*Perfectionism is at the heart
of all human neurosis.*
— Albert Ellis

Elvis rocked the charts with *Heartbreak Hotel, Hound Dog,* and *Hard Headed Woman. Dragnet, I Love Lucy,* and *Gunsmoke* rode the airwaves. People flocked to movie theaters to watch Marlon Brando in *On the Waterfront,* Marilyn Monroe in *Some Like It Hot,* Gary Cooper in *High Noon.*

But, in the Indiana of the nineteen-fifties, where I grew up, basketball reigned king. On both weekend and weekday nights, Hoosiers packed gymnasiums across the state, stomping, cheering, and clapping for their favorite team. Basketball hoops stood tall and regal in every neighborhood, whether it be a city, town, or hamlet. Sports pages headlined each game and golden-throated announcers in high-pitched voices described the play-by-play action to families huddled around their living room radios. To be a basketball player in Indiana was to be a warrior, to live a dream, to be a hero.

It started for me when I was ten.[1] I came home from school one chilly fall afternoon to find a wooden backboard, replete with a metal basket and a chain net, nailed to the garage behind my house. With its door rolled up, a player would complete his lay-up next to our lawnmower, barbecue grill, and deflated wading pool.

Spotting me through the kitchen window, Dad came outside dribbling a brand-new leather basketball that would become scuffed and discolored in a matter of weeks. With a wide grin on his face, he bounced the ball to me and said, "Let's play some ball."

My first efforts to shoot the ball through the basket were awkward and feckless. I pushed the ball straight-arm from my chest, banging my first attempt off the front of the rim, the second straight into the garage, and the third against the backboard without touching iron. Ten minutes in, I had yet to come close to making a basket and could feel frustration and discouragement welling up inside me.

"This is stupid," I said, after I bricked yet another shot.

"Here, let me show you how it's done," Dad said. "You'll get it."

He dribbled the ball out to me and faced the basket. "Don't push the ball—flick it with your wrist," he said, demonstrating the technique without shooting. "The flick produces backspin and gives a softness to the shot."

Then he took a couple of shots while I rebounded for him. Each time he talked me through what he was doing, and each time the ball found the net.

"There," he said, again bouncing the ball to me.

I shot the ball again, this time with a wrist flick and some arch, then again, and again. On the fourth try the ball plopped through the net with a jingle. I looked at Dad and smiled.

"How'd that feel?" he asked.

"Good."

"Yeah, like nothing else in the world," he said. "Keep shooting."

I did, missing many, but, like a rat in a Skinner Box, hitting just enough to encourage me to keep trying. The more I shot, the more I made. The more I made, the better the ball's leather felt in my hands, the more compelling the thump, thump, thump of my dribbling sounded, the greater my gratification when I rattled the net.

That day flowed into hundreds of others over the next few years. It wasn't long before the sounds of the basketball called forth the boys in the neighborhood—Larry, Jim, Harold, Eddie, and others whose names I can't recall but whose faces I can still picture. We played and we played—one-on-one, two-on-two, three-on-three—the first team to make twenty-one baskets being the winner.

Over time, I realized that I could play basketball better than the other boys in the neighborhood. Whenever I wanted, I could push my last dribble hard to the pavement, stop on a dime, elevate high into the air, release the ball at the top of my leap, and, as it dropped through the basket, hold the gooseneck pose with my right forearm and hand until I settled back to the concrete. I could drive hard to the basket and kiss a running left- or right-handed hook off the backboard and through the rim. I could leap high in the air when a teammate missed a shot to gently tap the ball into the basket before settling back onto the court. Gradually, without conscious awareness, I came to meld the playing of basketball with a sense of myself as a basketball player.

It was in the eighth grade that I first played organized ball. The Christ the King Monarchs played in the Diocese of Evansville Parochial League against other Catholic schools—Sacred Heart, Holy Rosary, St. Theresa, and the others.

That was when I first started experiencing anxiety. I would awaken on game day with a knot that gripped my mid-section until the referee tossed the ball into the air for tip-off. My dad told me it was "normal game day jitters," that it was part of every athlete's life. "Sweet agony," he called it.

In high school, I led my Bosse Bulldog freshman team to the city championship before being promoted to the varsity to finish out the season. There, on a bitter January night in 1957, I stood at mid-court in the lay-up line, surrounded by thousands of people about to watch me play basketball. Around the court, the stomping and clapping and cheering thundered; the colors of scarlet and gray, gold and purple swirled in the stands; the air smelled of sweat and popcorn. Wearing number twenty-two on my brand new white uniform, I ran the lay-up line with my heart pounding, my stomach full of jitters, my reflexes so coiled I could have jumped over the backboard if somebody yelled "boo" in my ear.

Once in action, my nerves calmed and I settled into the game. The players ran faster, passed the ball sharper, bumped with more force and vigor than I was accustomed. But I forgot my age, my inexperience, and the hubbub around me, eventually scoring eight points that night. Then I scored in double digits in each game for the rest of that season.

Come my sophomore year, I started strong, scoring between fourteen and seventeen points in my first four games. Following my fifth game, the drumbeat started—first on the outside, then on the inside—when the *Evansville Courier* headlined my name in giant black letters: "GRIEGER PACES BOSSE'S 79–37 VICTORY OVER BOONVILLE." The sports writer Jack Schneider wrote:

> With brilliant sophomore forward Russ Grieger spearheading the charge, Bosse romped past Boonville,
> 79–37, last night at Central Gym.
> Grieger, displaying the kind of finesse and
> shooting accuracy that belies his tender age and lack of experience, scored 23 points, including nine field goals in 14 shots.
>
> Young Russ connected on his first three field goals attempts, helping Bosse spurt to a 13–2 lead after four minutes and a 23–3 advantage at the end of the opening period.
>
> And after the Bulldogs bogged down a bit in the
> second quarter when the Pioneers played them on even

terms, Grieger got them back on the right track again in his 14 shots.

Following the intermission, the 6'1" youngster scored 10 points and hit four of his five shots before leaving the game with two and one half minutes left in the third frame. He sat out the rest of the game.

My fifteen-year-old mind barely had time to digest all of this when the same Jack Schneider laid it on even thicker. On January 27, 1958, he wrote:

It would be foolhardy to underestimate the potential of this Bosse team. The Bulldogs have size, speed, and scoring ability. They are rapidly accumulating the only ingredient they weren't well stocked with when the season began—experience. And they have one of the greatest young prospects in the city's hardwood history in 6'1" sophomore Russ Grieger who already may be the very finest among the present crop of Evansville prep cagers. Grieger displays the kind of finesse and shooting accuracy that belies his tender age and lack of experience. He is averaging almost 14 points per game and is the leading scorer on the team. But more indicative of his effectiveness has been his brilliant shooting. In the ten games played, young Russ scored 52 field goals for a blazing .509 percent.

I sat at the breakfast table, reading the paper, oblivious to Mom clinking plates and silverware in the kitchen. I fixated on one sentence: *"And they may have one of the greatest young prospects in the city's hardwood history in 6'1" sophomore Russ Grieger who already may be the very finest among the present crop of Evansville prep cagers."*

I looked at Mom. She smiled, then continued her kitchen chores.

Right then it hit me—a feeling of dread that came from a place I could not put into words. It was a sense of being watched, shadowed, all eyes on me, waiting to see if I would measure up to these expectations. My stomach felt as if somebody had thrust a hand inside me and squeezed with all their might.

"Oh, God," I said out loud.

If pregame jitters represented the youth of my emotional struggles, that moment marked their growth into maturity. It was the moment when my focus shifted from pleasure to performance. But I was not driven to perform well in order to reap the euphoria of the sport itself. I was driven by the necessity to perform well, to prove myself worthy to others, as if my life depended on it. Instead of looking upon basketball as a passion, I perverted it into a game of desperate perfection. *I have to do well and look good or else* became my motivation. With that new perspective came fear of failure, of judgment, of humiliation.

When tormented, you run. Some run faster and harder, in an all-out effort to achieve perfectionism. Others run away—avoiding, procrastinating, calling in sick. Still others slow down, scale back, try to meld into the background. That's what I did. Outside of my conscious awareness, I reasoned that, if I were to put out to the best of my ability and then fail, it would shame me; but, if I didn't put out, then I wouldn't actually fail. I had an excuse. I would then be spared the shame of displaying to the whole world what a failure I was.

For the next four games, I coasted at three-quarter speed as if I carried ten-pound weights on each of my shoulders. I didn't thrust hard past a screen to get open for a shot, power drive to the basket for a lay-up, claw at my defender as if he held the magic elixir that would save my life. I let other players drive the action, following along passively as if in a drug-induced stupor.

My paltry production mirrored my slovenly effort, both of which caught the attention of the media, my coach, and my father. "You okay?" Dad asked.

"Yeah."

"You sure?"

"Yeah."

On the Monday after that fourth game, my coach stuck his head into my third-period class to take me to his second-floor office adjacent to the cramped gym where we practiced. He slowly scooted his whistle that was attached to what looked like a soiled shoestring to the side. He then rested his hands palm-up on the desktop and looked me in the eye. I felt like I was waiting for a jury foreman to announce the verdict in my murder trial.

After what seemed like an eternity, he said, "Things pretty rough for you, aren't they."

"Yeah, I guess so," I said.

"Look, Russ," he said, "you haven't been yourself for a few weeks now. I can see it. You've been going through the motions."

I sat silent, feeling vulnerable, guilty.

He went on. "You're an outstanding basketball player and you will leave the school one of the best ever to wear a Bosse uniform. But you're only a sophomore. Don't expect so much of yourself. You can't always be on your game. Lighten up on yourself."

My eyes filled with tears, which I quickly brushed away with my shirtsleeve.

"One more thing," he said. "I don't care whether or not you score another point the rest of the season. Rebound, get the ball to the open man, play defense. Just forget what those guys wrote. Just play ball. Okay?"

"Okay," I said.

"Okay, then," he said, standing up, "Get back to class, and I'll see you this afternoon at practice."

I walked out of Coach's office feeling light and airy, as if a sinister vapor had been sucked out of my mid-section. I took the steps two at a time down to the first floor. Halfway to my classroom, I jumped up and feigned a jump shot into an imaginary basket. Once I walked into the classroom, I announced my return with an exultant "Ta-daaah!"

Three nights later, against the Vincennes Alices, I again ran the court with energy and chutzpah. I delighted in the hipping and elbowing that flourished under the basket, thrilled to the act of releasing the ball at the top of my jump and watching it sandpaper the net, grooved to the dance my teammates and I did as we ran our offense. The next morning's sports headline read, "GRIEGER EMERGES FROM HIS SLUMP." It reflected not only my performance on the court the night before, but my inner self as well.

Thank God for Coach Keller's psychotherapeutic wizardry. He rescued me from a season of emotional misery. Though I did not connect my perfectionistic thinking to my anxiety-driven avoidance of basketball failure then, I do now. I see that my perfectionism not only created anxiety for me in basketball, but in other areas of my high school life as well—in academics, with girls, in my social life in general.

And, now, as a practicing psychotherapist with over thirty years' experience, I clearly see that perfectionism is the root source of virtually all the emotional problems I see in my office. It comes in many forms—the anxieties, depressions, angers and hostilities, and shames and embarrassments, among others. Consequently, I know that, to relieve people of their emotional pain, I must help them relinquish their allegiance to perfectionism, just as Coach Keller tried to do with me.

With regard to **anxiety**, I think of twenty-three-year-old Corinne, a first-year graduate student at the University of Virginia pursuing her doctorate in astronomy. Not only does she drive herself to the point of exhaustion with her perfectionistic demand for straight A's, but she also regularly creates panic for herself, afraid that she'll fall short of her expectations and thereby ruin her perfect 4.0 grade point average.

On the other side of the anxiety coin are procrastination, indecision, and avoidance. I know of no better example of this than the brilliant South African novelist, essayist, and Nobel Prize recipient in Literature, J. M. Coetzee. In his 2002 memoir, *Youth: Scenes from Provincial Life II*, he writes about his creative block when he was a freshly settled twenty-something in England. It seemed that for nearly two years he lollygagged about without writing, waiting and hoping for inspiration to propel him into creativity. He didn't want to face the fact that he'd have to will himself to risk the possibility of failure, that unless he forced himself to act, nothing would happen.

Then, in a flash, he saw the truth:

> "What is wrong with him is that he is not prepared to fail. He wants an A or an alpha or one hundred percent for his every attempt, and a big Excellent! in the margin. Ludicrous! Childish! He does not have to be told so: he can see it for himself. Nevertheless. Nevertheless he cannot do it. Not today. Not tomorrow. Perhaps tomorrow he will be in the mood, have the courage."

Without uttering the words "perfect" or "perfection," you can almost hear those words coming off the page. If you carefully listen, he is saying to himself, without conscious awareness: *I must write perfectly and brilliantly. It would be horrible of me to fail at this. What a second-rate person I would prove to be.*

If anxiety has to do with fears about the future, then **depression** has to do with events in the past or present. With the belief, "I must never, ever fail at anything," forty-eight-year-old Catherine damned herself into a deep depression for failing to act perfectly in her ministry. She peppered her thinking with such damaging assertions as these: "I should have given a better sermon last Sunday." "I should have visited him in the hospital before he died." "I should have counseled that couple better." Nothing she did was good enough in her eyes, and she hated herself for it.

Then there was Clara, the mother of three, who perfectionistically thought that nothing she did was good enough. When she prepared a delicious stir-fry for supper, she damned herself for its commonness. After she taught Sunday Bible study at church, she drove home criticizing herself because her lessons lacked the depth she expected. Though she babysat her neighbor's children, she attacked herself for what she could have done to make their time more enjoyable, interesting, nurturing.

Both Catherine and Clara exemplify what we in REBT call *Self-Damning Depression*, the depression that results from a person damning himself or herself for failing to act perfectly. A second type of depression is what we call *Catastrophizing Depression*. In this, a person catastrophizes against life's hardships, as if life should be perfectly free of setbacks, hardships, even tragedies.

Twenty-five-year-old Scott valiantly fights Catastrophizing Depression. Burdened with an undetermined neurological disorder that periodically renders him so debilitated that he had to drop out of school for months on end, he still, in his sixth year in college, labors to complete his bachelor's degree. When he takes the attitude, "I hate this, but it is what it is," he gracefully lumps his lot and pushes on. But, when he falls into demanding perfection of his life, thinking, "I shouldn't have to deal with this," he falls into bitterness, self-pity, and depression.

Even **anger and hostility** are rooted in perfectionism, for such reactions come from demanding that other people must never act badly or make mistakes. Vic, for example, berated his wife for daring to suffer from alcoholism. He believed that she shouldn't be so weak and should control her drinking.

Similarly, Karen found it so difficult to control her anger toward her preschool twins that Social Services had to intervene. Her perfectionistic belief: "They shouldn't be so difficult and cause the ruckus they do."

And then there was Phil who railed against every slight or offense he encountered, whether at home, at work, or in random public places. His rationale: "They should know better!" "They should be more alert!" "They shouldn't have done that!"

Shame, embarrassment, and **guilt** are all similar in that they result from a person demanding perfect performance from themselves. For those who experience these painful emotions, to fail at something is thought to be so horrible and deplorable that one must hang one's head and avert one's eyes throughout eternity.

Mark is as good an example of this. In his early fifties, he is highly successful by all standards—a businessperson, champion club golfer, community leader. In one arena, however, he sees himself as a failure: he is twice-divorced and in the throes of a failing third marriage. There is so much ill-will, acrimony, and distrust between him and his wife that I see very little hope that they can mend their fences, much less find harmony and happiness together.

Yet Mark feels stuck in this acrimonious relationship, unable to summon the willpower to walk away. Why? Because he feels shame, embarrassment and guilt, all driven by his perfectionistic self-damnation.

He believes:	"There is something wrong with me to have failed now in three marriages."
The translation:	"I must not have any relationship flaws. To have them makes me a flawed, shameful person."
He believes:	"People will think I'm a real loser if I fail at this third marriage."
The translation:	"I must have perfect approval from all people who know me."
He believes:	"It would be horrible to fail at this marriage."
Translation:	"I must perfectly succeed in marriage, no matter how difficult and unfulfilling it may be."

The people I briefly describe are just a few of those I counsel who cause themselves misery from their perfectionistic thinking. Other emotional problems that arise from perfectionism include eating disorders, borderline personality disorders, substance abuse and dependency, marital disharmony and conflict, sexual dysfunction, and low frustration tolerance.

I can relate to all these struggling people, for I too have been there. If I had never fallen into the trap of perfectionism in high school, I would not only have experienced much less anxiety, but I probably would have been much more productive. If the patients I introduced above had not held their perfectionistic beliefs, they too would have had more happiness and success in their lives as well. If we could eliminate perfectionism across the universe, humanity would be transformed.

Reflection

I'd bet you dollars to donuts my high school basketball coach, Herman Keller, had never taken a psychotherapy class in his life. But, it is clear to me that he intuitively understood that my perfectionism crippled both my effort and my productivity. And, like a competent cognitive-behavior therapist, he did his best to rid me of that spirit-crushing way of thinking.

REBT seeks to do for its patients what Coach Keller did for me. By understanding that all perfectionism entails a person illogically concluding that, because I want to do well and be liked, be treated well, and find life to my liking, it absolutely must be so, it uses the Socratic method of repeated and persistent questioning. That is, it assists the patient in holding his or her perfectionistic beliefs up to skeptical scrutiny. The therapist helps the patient clearly see how illogical these beliefs are, how they cause harm to oneself and to others, what evidence there is to debunk them. Through such a sustained logical-empirical assault, self-defeating beliefs are gradually weakened and destroyed, thereby relieving the symptomatic feelings and behaviors, and opening the door to adopting more realistic, anti-perfectionistic ways of thinking.

In most cases, the patient has harbored his or her perfectionistic beliefs for years, sometimes even for decades. They are most often deeply endorsed and habituated. This makes it difficult for the patient to relinquish them. It therefore behooves both the therapist and the patient to be armed with the most powerful arguments against both their validity and their practicality. What follows are the major arguments I have collected against the validity of all perfectionistic demands, whether they are directed toward oneself, another, or the circumstances in life.

A first argument is that they are **NOT IN OUR BEST INTERESTS**. They directly cause the emotional miseries illustrated earlier, as well as most all other aberrant and self-defeating behaviors. They thus interfere with both happiness and productivity.

Another important argument against perfectionistic demands is that they are **UNREASONABLE**. It is simply impossible to always do well and always be liked, no matter how hard we try. We are all fallible, talented mistake makers, and erring on occasion is inevitable. Similarly, no other human being can possibly always act correctly. He or she is also fallible and imperfect, and therefore will inevitably act at times rotten, pig-headed, or inept. And it is impossible for the things in the world, whether they be machines, institutions, or events, to always function to the full extent of their capacity. Everything is in potential breakdown and will ultimately fail. So, preferring that I, you, or things behave correctly is reasonable, for who in their right mind would really want to goof or to run into hardships. But, to demand that I, you, or things always go smoothly flies in the face of reasonableness. It is impossible, and it just sets us up for misery when, inevitably, I, you, or it break down.

A further argument against perfectionistic demands is that they **CONTRADICT REALITY**. Reality is the way it is. How can one claim they are thinking rationally when they say, "I shouldn't have done that!"? Or, "You shouldn't have goofed!"? Or, "It should have gone better!"? We may agree that it was bad, that it would be a lot better if it weren't the way it is, that it would be most desirable to change it or try to prevent it from recurring in the future. But, how can we say that it shouldn't be the way it actually is, when it is, in fact, that way?

Why would I be so critical of the demand that something shouldn't be the way it is? The answer lies in the conviction that we live in a causal universe. That is, events occur when and only when the conditions necessary to cause those events are present. Things don't just happen for no reason. They happen because the necessary antecedent circumstances are present to make them happen.

Take, for example, the space shuttle that exploded and killed the astronauts a number of years ago. Common wisdom is that it shouldn't have happened. But, to the contrary, while it was deplorable, it should have happened, when you think causally. All the conditions necessary for it to happen—the quality of the parts of the shuttle, the engineering of the shuttle, the weather, and so on—were such that the explosion had to happen. There was nothing else that could have happened, given the conditions, and if the conditions were replicated, the same exact outcome would take place, at the same time, with the same results. So the space shuttle tragedy should have happened, causally speaking.

Fundamentally, the same idea of causation applies to all other events, including human behavior and emotions. We act, and others act, because the conditions that prevail at the time cause our behavior. It is only sometime later, after something goes wrong, that we then say, "I shouldn't have done that!" Back when we did it, we didn't think, "I guess I'll go make a big mistake now." No, we acted as we did given the causal conditions at that time, including our knowledge base. Therefore, we can't very well defend the statement, "I shouldn't have done what I did." But we almost certainly could defend a number of preferential alternatives such as: "I wish I hadn't done that," "It would be a lot better if I hadn't done what I did," "I don't like what happened and I hope I can prevent its recurrence." With such preferential statements, we have the best of both worlds: on the one hand, we own responsibility for our actions, such that we can make needed changes; on the other hand, we do not cause ourselves the agony of emotional disturbance.

A fourth argument against perfectionistic demands is that they are both **ILLOGICAL** and **EGOTISTICAL**. If you think about it, you will see that all demands say: "Because I prefer this, it should be that way!" First, this does not logically make sense any more than saying that "Because I want it to be sunny, it should be." These are non-sequiturs—the conclusion simply does not follow from the premise. Second, we do not run the universe! It is pretty grandiose for us to say that what we want—to succeed, to be loved, to be treated well, to have things work out—must be granted. The universe, in fact, is impersonal. As far as we know, not only does it not care about us, it doesn't even know we exist.

A fifth argument against perfectionistic demands is that they **FALSELY IMPLY UNIVERSAL IMPERATIVES**. A demand suggests that an absolute, inviolate law exists that commands a certain outcome, whether that be our own perfection, that of another, or that of the universe. For me to claim, for example, that you must understand and agree with the ideas I am presenting suggests that there is some force in the universe that commands you to do so. The plain truth is that there are no universal laws or imperatives that force this outcome. In fact, if you think about it, if there were such an imperative, then you would have no choice but to swallow everything I communicate; you would have to automatically agree with me. The fact that you may disagree shows in and of itself that there is no law compelling you to agree. You simply could not disagree if you really had to agree.

A sixth argument against perfectionistic demands is that they **FALSELY IMPLY NECESSITY**. Demands, in other words, say: "I need to do well, to be liked, to be treated well by you, to get everything I want in life." But "need" means, if you really think about it, that it is a matter of life and death to get what is desirable; if what I want or prefer does not come about, then I will die. Isn't that silly. We only need, really need, what sustains our life, the basics: food, air, shelter, and water. The truth is that we do not need almost all the things we want. Everything else is only desirable, adding to the quality of life. We humans would be wise to get rid of this "need" idea and simply accept that we can still have relative happiness when we are frustrated in some of our desires.

A seventh argument against perfectionistic demands is that they almost always **EXAGGERATE THE BADNESS OF EVENTS OUT OF PERSPECTIVE**. For, if it is true that I, you, or life must be perfect, then it follows that it is awful, horrible, or terrible for me, you, or life to fall short. Think about it: when we "awfulize" about something, don't we mean that this undesirable or bad thing is close to, if not actually, the worst thing that could ever happen? Isn't it true, though, that, while there are a few things that could rate somewhere between ninety and one hundred percent bad, say genocide, child abuse, or racism, almost everything that goes wrong in our lives falls into the realm of one to twenty percent bad. So, when we demand perfection, we tend to exaggerate the badness of failure, mistreatment, or frustration, thereby further upsetting ourselves and, then, unfortunately, reinforcing in our minds the correctness of thinking perfectionistically in the first place.

Eighth and last, perfectionistic demands set us up for **SELF-DAMNING**. For, if there is a universal law commanding us, another person, or life to be perfect, then it follows that I, you, or life are damnable for failing. But, this illogically fails to discriminate between the failing performance and the whole person. To totally damn myself, you, or life for failing at one thing would be as illogical as destroying a Stradivarius violin because one string broke.

I want to conclude this discussion by saying that there is both good news and bad news. The bad news is that our human mind easily thinks along these perfectionistic lines. Though the concept, "I want to do well," is quite distinct from the concept, "I must do perfectly well," it is beyond tempting for we humans to illogically conclude: "Because I want to do well, I must perfectly do so." "Because I want you to treat me well, you must do so." "Because I want the circumstances in my life to be good, they must be." It is thereby easy to make ourselves anxious, depressed, angry, and guilt-ridden.

But there is also good news. It is that we humans need not be the helpless victims of our own human mind. We can, if we so decide, observe our own thinking, critically analyze its validity—logically, empirically, and practically—and choose to only believe and act only on what proves to be true based on logic, empirical evidence, and practical usefulness.

This, I argue, is the purpose of all good psychotherapy. It is what we want to teach all our patients to do on their own, thereby helping them become their own psychotherapist. It is what we want to impart to our children. It is the wise thing for all of us to practice in our own personal lives. The goal is for all of us to accept ourselves as perfectly imperfect and thereby to be free to pursue happiness.

Note

1 A fuller description of this can be found in my memoir, *The Perfect Season: A Memoir of the 1964–1965 Evansville College Purple Aces*. Bloomington: Indiana University Press, 2016.

Reference

Coetzee, J. M. (2002). *Youth: Scenes from Provincial Life II*. New York: Penguin.

10

HAPPINESS ON PURPOSE

If it's going to be, it's up to me

> *The purpose of our lives*
> *is to be happy.*
> *— The 14th Dalai Lama*

Although I was a full-blooded jock and frat boy in college, I often hung out with the theater crowd. They provided me with a degree of refinement and intellectual stimulation that balanced my raucous education in the locker room and smoke-filled pubs throughout the city.

On many weekend nights, I'd dress in black slacks and shirt, assume my best brooding demeanor, and sit cross-legged on the floor of one of their apartments. With lamps glowing softly, jazz music playing in the background, and beer and wine emboldening us, we'd mull over the perplexities of life by the hour. The conversation drifted from Stanislavski's method acting to the character flaws of Othello to the difference between Elizabethan and modern tragedy. I'd mostly sit and listen, interjecting a thought on occasion, all the while feeling soulful, sophisticated, and bohemian.

The topic that fascinated me above all others was the Existentialists' notion that life is absurd and meaningless, about nothing. We found evidence of this in the novels of Dostoyevsky and Kafka and the philosophies of Kierkegaard, Sartre, and especially Camus. Not the most cheerful of subjects, I admit, but, in our young minds, the fact that we pondered such weighty issues gave us a sense that we had substance, that our lives mattered.

I was in my early twenties. What seemed so romantically bleak back then has now taken on a whole new caste for me—one of hope and power, even elation. The fact that life may have no intrinsic purpose can provide us the freedom to create our own purpose. It can define our own existence. Rather than follow the pre-ordained path anointed upon us by a higher power or the mold dictated by the vagaries of society, we are free to make something out of nothing.

And so, if there is any validity to all this, the question becomes: What is the best goal we should strive toward? What purpose is worth spending our time and energy to pursue? Maybe the answer lies in what the Dalai Lama says: "The purpose of our lives is to be happy." Maybe the ultimate purpose of psychotherapy is to help people experience precisely that.

No one illustrates this more clearly than one of my patients, thirty-eight-year-old Kelly. The first words out of her mouth when she walked into my office were, "I hate myself."

"What makes you hate yourself?" I asked, more than willing to get right to the heart of her troubles.

"This," she said, motioning with her hands to showcase her body.

What she exhibited, Vanna White-style, was a five-foot-five-inch body that carried well over three hundred pounds. With three chins stacked down her neck, a stomach that protruded out farther than her ample chest, and large amounts of loose flesh hanging from her underarms, her girth took up three-quarters of the loveseat.

"So, Kelly, you're depressed about your weight, right?"

"Yes."

"And I gather that you're depressed about your weight because you've gone from telling yourself, first, that you hate your body to, second, that you hate yourself for it. Am I correct?"

"Exactly."

"But, Kelly," I said in classic REBT fashion, "hating yourself is exactly the reason why you're depressed. Why not just hate your body and then, if you want, do something about it, like lose weight? Why generalize from your body to your entire self, your whole personhood, to you, the owner of your body?"

She looked at me with a furrowed brow and a downward tilt of her face. "But aren't they one and the same?"

"No way," I said. "Here, let me show you visually."

I then drew a large circle on the whiteboard perched on an easel to my right, tapped twenty or so dots inside it, and said, "Look, Kelly, the circle represents you and these dots, plus many, many more, represent every characteristic you possess—good, bad, indifferent. Your body is just one of the dots like this one here," I said, circling one of them.

"Okay?"

"So, how logical is it to generalize from this one dot, representing your body, to the whole circle, which is you?"

Kelly paused, staring at the whiteboard. Finally, she said, "I guess it's not."

"No, it's not," I said. "It's an illogical overgeneralization, like throwing out your whole wardrobe if one of your blouses is soiled. But that's the way you automatically think about yourself. It's okay, maybe even good, to damn the dot, because it could motivate you to lose weight. But it's insane to damn your whole self."[1]

This exchange, lasting maybe ten minutes, completed my REBT diagnosis of Kelly's depression. It provided her the insight that her irrational self-damning had caused her depression, and pointed her

Over the course of the next several weeks, Kelly and I repeatedly went over the illogic of her conviction that she was a hateful person. We capped each disputation with a rational self-accepting alternative.

One day, a couple of months into her psychotherapy, Kelly walked into my office, grinning like a schoolgirl bursting to reveal a secret. She stopped in front of the loveseat and faced me, opened her arms wide with her palms up, displaying her whole body, and said, "I got it, Dr. Grieger."

"Yeah, what?" I said, eager to hear what she had to say.

"What you see here in front of you is not me. What you see here is just my body. I'm so much bigger than my body."

"Wow," I said, my eyes wide and alive. "Do you really know that to be true?"

"I not only know it, but I believe it," she said, sitting down on the couch behind her. "I haven't felt a second's depression for almost a week now."

"That's wonderful, Kelly. So, what's it feel like to not be depressed?"

She paused for a few seconds, her eyes gazing blankly into the middle distance. Then she said, "Like, happy, I guess. If this is what it feels like to be happy, I want more of it."

"Awesome," I said.

Kelly looked me right in the eye, a sincere, pleading look. "Will you help me do that? Be happy?"

"I thought you'd never ask," I said, grinning my biggest grin. "Let's get right to it."

Kelly didn't know it, but I had thought about the concept of happiness for years, searching through the writings of philosophers, scholars, and theologians who pondered the purpose of life long before and after the Existentialists. Why are we here? What are we put here to do? What is our purpose?

No one really knows definitively the answers to these questions. But I want to suggest that there are strong arguments to support the notion that the purpose of life is to be happy. Aristotle supplied us the logic. He observed that virtually every goal we humans set ultimately serves the purpose of being happy. We strive to mate with a person with whom we can share mutual love. For what purpose? To be happy. We save money in order to secure a good retirement. But why? The answer is to end up happy. We lead a virtuous life so that, after we die, we can spend eternity in heaven with God. What for? For happiness.

So, every goal or desire we have, rather than an end in itself, serves the ultimate goal of being happy. The one exception is happiness. There is no goal beyond itself for which happiness serves. We don't strive to be happy in order to find a loving mate, or to secure a good retirement, or even in order to spend an eternity in heaven. No, happiness does not have an "in order to …" after it. It is the ultimate end of everything else.

That's Aristotle's logic. But there's also anthropological evidence to back him up. It seems that, if we look across all cultures and societies, all humans, no matter what their race, creed, or color, share two fundamental drives. One is to survive. The second is, while surviving, to be happy. Honestly, have you ever known a person who doesn't naturally crave these two outcomes?

So, if happiness is the purpose of life, the challenge then is to define exactly what happiness is. Is it a feeling state? Is it a condition that results from checking off all of our cherished goals? Is it a way of being in the world? If we don't know what happiness is, how can we strive to achieve it?

After long and hard thought, I take the liberty to offer the following definition of happiness. Notice, as you read it, that happiness has to do with something much deeper than merely experiencing positive feeling states. Notice also that happiness has to do with action—acting, being engaged, purposely doing what one finds important. And, notice that happiness does not refer to an accidental by-product of the circumstances in life aligning to one's liking. Rather, happiness comes from deep qualities within that provide the proper structure and direction to life. Here's my definition:

> *Happiness is acting in accordance*
> *with your passionate purpose,*
> *grounded in rational thought and*
> *self-discipline, and guided by*
> *ethical principles.*

An intriguing definition, isn't it? And, I assert, a useful one as well. Let me break it down into its component parts so that you can put it to practical use in your life.

Happiness. Pleasure refers to a positive experience at a given moment in time. For example, I might say, "I enjoyed the movie." Or, "It was wonderful to share Thanksgiving with my family." Or, "What a wonderful vacation we had." These feeling states are positive, but transitory, coming and going over time, much like the weather. Happiness, to the contrary, is much more than a series of pleasures; it has to do with the overall quality of life as a whole. With emotional highs and lows a given for everyone, a truly happy person is one who can generally say that life is rewarding and satisfying, who experiences a life in which one prospers and flourishes, who lives a life which one loves to live. A happy person is one who finds life to be meaningful and significant.

Acting. Acting has two meanings with regard to happiness. It means, first, that a person must actually engage in the actions that are necessary to bring about happiness. In other words, one must do what's necessary to be happy, rather than sitting back and hoping, wishing, or praying that a happy state will come knocking on the front door. But the second meaning of acting goes much deeper and is more profound. It means that, to be truly happy, one must consistently engage in activities that have profoundly personal significance to oneself.

Passionate Purpose. It is obvious, I hope, that not just any actions will bring about a truly happy life. After all, ants constantly keep busy. It is when one aligns one's action with a passionate purpose for living that one has the potential to rise in the morning full of energy and eager for the day, then puts one's head on the pillow at night feeling fulfilled, satisfied, and, yes, happy.

Rational Thought. Unfortunately, there are sinister forces arrayed against us that threaten to derail our ability to live our passionate purpose. Not the least of which is our fallible human mind that all too readily thinks irrationally, thereby creating the kinds of negative emotions—anger, anxiety, guilt, depression—that can block our path to happiness. The bottom line is that rational thought prompts happiness, while irrational thought undercuts happiness. It's as simple—and profound—as that.

Self-Discipline. Isn't it ironic how life finds ways to devil us, often without bothering to give us fair warning? One way is when life forces us to choose between, on the one hand indulging in some immediate pleasure that can bring us harm in the long run and, on the other hand suffering short-range frustration by delaying gratification for more happiness in the long run. When these two are in conflict, many people opt for the immediate, thereby damaging their chance for happiness in the long run. For one to be happy, it is imperative to possess the ability to put aside immediate gratification when it jeopardizes greater rewards in the long run.

Ethical Principles. The German Nazis acted passionately on what they thought to be a sacred purpose. Yet their ethics were so abysmal that words fail to capture their cruelty and depravity. To be happy means not only to act in order to live one's passionate purpose, but to do so in a manner that is guided by moral and ethical principles of the highest order.

So, this is what I have come to believe happiness is. One experiences happiness when consistently acting in accordance with a personally profound passionate purpose, grounded in rational thought and self-discipline, and guided by ethical principles. From both my personal and clinical experience, I believe that, by mastering these components of happiness, a person will find oneself filled with energy and enthusiasm each day, be productive across the breadth of life, and regularly experience satisfaction, fulfillment, and happiness.

Let us return once more to Kelly's story. After helping her with her depression, we set out on a quest for her to find happiness. Our first task was to define her passionate purpose. She initially struggled with that, being so conditioned to disparage herself. "I don't know if I have what it takes to do that," she said.

"Of course you do," I said. "Remember that you're bigger than any one part of you, and there's lots of space inside yourself to develop new skills and traits. I'll help you."

Through questioning and discussion, she gradually honed her life's purpose: "To be a passionate source of happiness, first to myself, and then to all the other people in my life as well."

I printed this statement on the whiteboard in big, bold letters. We both eyed it as if we were proud parents seeing our newborn infant for the first time. Finally, she sighed and asked, "Do you really think that can be me?"

"I do," I said. "Don't worry, I'll coach you through the process." I then asked her to "look one year into the future and imagine what your life would look like if it matched exactly your purpose statement."

After fits and starts, Kelly finally voiced the following, which I dutifully inscribed on the whiteboard:

1. Have no depression.
2. Weigh no more than two hundred pounds.
3. Be in a committed, romantic relationship.
4. Be regularly connected with family and friends.
5. Engage fully in treasured interests—quilting, reading, gardening.

Once she created her list, I fully expected Kelly to be excited about the vision of her future. Instead, she scrunched her face into a frown and said, "That looks so far out of my reach. How in the world will I ever make all that a reality?"

"With focus, and determination, and persistence," I said, "one day at a time. You can do it, and I'll guide you." I paused, then smiled. "By the way, Kelly, you're not my first rodeo, you know."

"Dr. Cliché," she said, smiling.

"You bet," I said. "Now let's get to work on creating the life you would love to live."

And we did. For each of her five goals, I instructed her to note one, two, or three actions she could take that would move her closer to her vision. Then I suggested she pick one thing she would do during the week before our next appointment to move closer to each goal. Here's what she committed to do:

1. Do my self-therapy daily.
2. Make an appointment with a nutritionist and a personal trainer.
3. Join an online dating service.
4. Call my sister in Kansas City.
5. Enroll in a quilting group.

I glanced at the clock and noticed our time together had come to an end. "You did great today, Kelly," I said. "Now your job is to follow through—no excuses, no matter what."

She walked out the door, with as massive a body as the day I first met her. Yet, today, I saw a woman strong of spirit and conviction, not the weak, helpless, despondent one who first walked into my office. I knew I'd have to continue to counsel her with regard to behaving with personal responsibility, fearlessness, and self-acceptance until she created the life she wanted. But, I had confidence that, if we both did our job, she'd find the happiness she craved.

Reflection

I intentionally titled this chapter Happiness on Purpose to stress that it takes committed, sustained action—**ON** purpose—to experience a sustained, happy life. This is true because there are at least three forces aligned against us that make it difficult to create and sustain a happy life. One force that stands against us, as Voltaire says, is that, "This is not the best of all possible worlds." No matter who we are, life challenges each of us with a steady stream of annoyances, frustrations, and deprivations—and, yes, sometimes, tragedies. This is the lot we all share.

Secondly, we do not live among saints or angels. Rather, we live alongside imperfect, fallible human beings who frequently act foolishly and on occasion even treat us less than sterling. Whether close or distant to us, they regularly commit (1) sins of commission, by doing things we don't like, and (2) sins of omission, by not doing things we do like. And here's the kicker: not only will people act badly, they will do so when they do, whether it's convenient to us or not. Such is life.

If that's not enough, there's a third factor that works against our happiness: we operate with the human mind. As wonderful as are the gifts our mind gives us—the capacity for abstract thought, the ability to communicate, the experience of love, our sense of humor, an opportunity to appreciate art and music—we are not innately gifted with the ability to consistently use our minds well. We find it all too easy to choose fiction over fact, distort reality, selectively attend to certain memories while ignoring others, exaggerate degrees of badness, and conclude that a certain desired outcome is absolutely necessary when in fact it is not. These distortions and irrationalities present quite a challenge in our quest for happiness.

All three of these challenges are part of the human condition and pose obstacles to our happiness. But, as I tell my patients, do not despair, for millions of people have overcome them. They have left clues. Imagine them having hiked through a forest and sprinkled M&Ms here and there to tell us the path to follow, leaving markers where a briar patch might tear our flesh or indicating ravines where we might fall.

This leads me to another reason I titled this chapter, Happiness on Purpose. The title suggests that happiness comes about when a person takes committed, sustained action that is on **_PURPOSE_**. This means to purposely live by five happiness principles:

1. *This Is It.* Today is all we have. Tomorrow might be no different or better. Besides, no one knows for certain that they'll even have a tomorrow. The bottom line: our time on earth is limited, so remind yourself of that every day so that you consciously and intentionally seek happiness at every turn.
2. *If It's Going to Be, It's Up to Me.* Nobody is put on this earth to make sure we are happy. Our happiness is not the responsibility of our significant other, our parents, our children, our friends, or our colleagues. Simply said, our happiness is our responsibility—one hundred percent, totally, no holds barred. Accept it. Embrace it. Act as if it's true.
3. *Decide to Be Happy.* Think of the major decisions you've made that have affected the rest of your life: where you chose to

go to college; who you married; your career choice. Trace the impact of these decisions on your life. I'll bet that the ripples of these decisions still reverberate today. Another decision I suspect you've not consciously made is whether or not to be happy. Determine that happiness is your goal and to commit to seek happiness throughout the fabric of your life.

4. *Act on Purpose.* You may possess all the trappings of happiness—health, money, physical attractiveness, power, status—but you will cripple your ability to be happy unless you act. As with Kelly, your actions have to include: (1) the creation of a passionate purpose, (2) the development of goals that serve the expression of that purpose, and (3) the elimination of irrational, self-indulgent, and unethical beliefs from your mind, so that you can adopt more rational, self-enhancing, and ethical ones to guide behavior and decisions.

5. *Work, Work, Work.* Simply hoping and praying to experience happiness is foolhardy. Try sitting in front of a TV and wishing the lawn gets cut. You need to get up and do it. As with the lawn, being happy isn't a one-time job. You must act *ON* purpose on *PURPOSE* for the rest of your life.

So, while appreciating how difficult it can be to lead a happy life, and with the commitment to teaching these five happiness principles, I assert that we REBT psychotherapists are nicely positioned to promote happiness in our patients. We can do that through what I call the Happiness Action Plan (HAP).[2] It lays out thirty happiness action strategies—ten to bring about happiness with oneself, ten for happiness with others, and ten for happiness with life in general—that can be used in total or customized to meet a patient's particular needs.

Happiness with Self

Cognitive Strategies	Behavioral Strategies
• Unconditional Self-Acceptance	• Gift Yourself Daily
• Appreciate Your Good Qualities	• Take Care of Your Body
• Be Perfectly Imperfect	• Speak Up for Yourself
• Want, Don't Need	• Take Time to Savor
• Refuse to Self-Pity	• Lighten Up and Laugh

Happiness with Others

Cognitive Strategies	Behavioral Strategies
• Accept and Forgive Others	• Choose Friends/Lovers Wisely
• Take Nothing Personal	• Be a Relentless Giver
• Be Generous of Spirit	• Listen, Listen, Listen
• Don't Be Needy	• Practice Win-Win
• Expect Misbehavior	• Leave a Trail of Happiness

Happiness with Life

Cognitive Strategies	Behavioral Strategies
• Hold Nothing Necessary	• Serve Yourself a Slice of Happiness
• Practice Perspective	• Rid Life's Unnecessary Negatives
• Practice Gratitude	• Practice Breakthroughs, Not Breakdowns
• Gracefully Lump Feel-Bads	• Make Friends with Death
• Treasure Today as a Gift	• Practice Curiosity

There it is—the path to happiness. Hark back to Aristotle who said that happiness is the goal behind every other goal a human has. People seek to fulfill specific goals with the hope, conscious or not, that their attainment will lead to greater happiness, not the other way around. I conclude that we mental health professionals have two profound responsibilities: one, to help free people from the emotional contamination and behavioral compulsions that create their misery; and, two, to assist people, once freed, to pursue happy, fulfilled lives.

Notes

1 See Chapter 5, Destroy Self-Esteem, for a full discussion of the irrationality of self-esteem toward a cognitive re-education that would lead to her cure.
2 The interested reader can turn to my *Psychology Today* blog, Happiness on Purpose, for a posting on each of these thirty items of the Happiness Action Plan.

EPILOGUE

It is early Friday morning, May 2, 2017. I sit at my dining room table. It is made of pine, thick and sturdy, with beveled circular legs that could have been modeled from those of a linebacker. Spring sunlight squeezes between tree branches outside the window to cut slender yellow ribbons over my notepad. The delicious smells of breakfast—cinnamon toast, bacon, hot chocolate—float to me from the kitchen. Many years have passed since that spring day in 1970 when I clenched my Ph.D. diploma on the turf of Ohio Stadium. Today I look forward to my first appointment at nine o'clock. A few minutes beforehand, I'll turn on the lamps to their softest wattage so that the lighting will be cozy and inviting. I'll sit at my desk and glance around, making sure everything is in place—my chair facing the loveseat on which my patients sit, compact boxes of Kleenex waiting to be used, a whiteboard resting on an easel should I find it important to outline the Contextual ABCs.

With a nod of my head that serves as my starter's pistol, I'll snap open my can of Diet Coke, step out to the waiting room, and invite my first patient into my office. This person suffers from PTSD. Two of the next three struggle with depression, the third, a married couple, find themselves deep in anger and conflict.

I feel energized. My goal will be to steer these people from enslavement to freedom. I know that, with my grasp of the fundamental nature of being human, and armed with my passionate purpose, I can understand them, enlighten them, show them the way forward to a better life. I know I'll give them my all.

I realize that I still have so much more to learn. I commit to keeping my mind open, not only by listening to what they tell me about themselves, but also to what they can teach me about human nature, how best to be of benefit to the people in my care, what I can further understand about myself as a person and a psychotherapist. I know that becoming a psychotherapist is a—never-ending journey.

INDEX

ABC model 7, 10–11, 23
acceptance (premeditated acceptance and forgiveness) 60–4
acting 160–1
alcoholics 115–20
Amber 115–21
anger 147; Greg 60–4
anxiety 75–9
arguments against perfectionism 149–54
Aristotle 159, 167

bargain basement shopping 55
B_B (general beliefs), 15
Being 82–5
Being at Cause 96–8, 101, 103–5
Being at Effect 96–7, 101–3
Beth 3–4
Betty 75
Beverly 134
The Bhagavad Gita 107
Billie 3
Borderline Personality Disorder 113
Boyd, John 85
B_P (paradynamic beliefs) 15
Brian 10, 92–6
B_T (situationally specific beliefs) 15

Catastrophizing 24n5
Catastrophizing Depression 49, 146
Catherine 146
causation 151
Charles 102–3

A Christmas Carol 65
Cicero, Marcus Tullius 107
Clara 146
Coetzee, J. M. 145
cognitive creation of consequences 17–18
cognitive creation of reality 16–17
cognitive-philosophic cure 18–22
compassion 67–73
Conditional Personal Responsibility 100, 102
consequences, cognitive creation of consequences 17–18
Contextual ABC Model 17
contextual nature of human cognition 12–16
Corinne 144–5
Covey, Stephen 33, 37, 42, 73
creating 32
creating purpose 40–1
Csikszentmihalyi, Mihaly 33
Cycle of Life 81

Dalai Lama 156
Daryl 67–72
depression: Catastrophizing Depression 49, 146 Self-Damning Depression 49, 146
destroy self-esteem xiii, 75–90
destroying happiness 86–7
discomfort, fears of 54–5
discovering 32
Doing 82–5
Don 111–15

elegance xiii, 123–31
Ellis, Albert 4–9, 23, 39, 52, 56n1, 137
embarrassment 147
emotional disturbance 23
enthusiasm 36–7
Erhard, Werner 92
Erhard Sensitivity Training (est) 91
ethical principles 161–2
Evaluative Beliefs 24n4
est 91
eye contact 93–4

failure, fears of 52–4
fearlessness xiii, 45–55
Fears of Discomfort 54–5
Fears of Failure 52–4
flow 33–4
forgiveness, (premeditated acceptance and forgiveness), interpersonal intelligence 60–4
Fred 104
freedom, psychological freedom 107–21

Gandhi, Mahatma 40–1, 108
Gary 3
generosity, Interpersonal Intelligence 65–7
Gibbs, Joe 57
goals 32
goodwill 57–9
Grabel, Paul 39
Greg 60–4
Grieger, Russell 139–44
grief 67–73
guilt 147

HAP (Happiness Action Plan) 166–7
happiness: definition of 160, destroying 86–7
Happiness Action Plan (HAP) 166–7
happiness on purpose xiii, 155–68

happiness principles 165–6
Heather 67–72, 75
Hegel, G. W. F. 107–8
High Frustration Tolerance 24n5
hostility, perfectionism 147
human cognition 12–16

Interpersonal Intelligence xiii, 59; compassion 67–73; generosity 65–7; premeditated acceptance and forgiveness 60–4; trust 73
interpersonal skills 58–9
irrational thinking 51

Jim 27–8
Joyce 5–8
Julie 75

Karen 147
Kathy 12–22
Keller, Herman 143–4, 148
Kelly 156–8, 162–4
Kevin 92, 108–11, 120
Krzyzewski, Mike 40

Laura 2–3, 108–110
Lauren 75
Laurie 133
Lawrence, T. E. 25
living your purpose 42–4
Locke, John 88, 107
Low Frustration Tolerance 24n5

make war on perfectionism xiii, 137–48; arguments against perfectionism 149–54
Margaret 26, 41
Mark 147–8
McCutchan, Arad 39
McGeady, Sister Mary Rose 123
Mead, Margaret 75–8
Michael 29–32
Molly 104

nature of being human xii, 1–11, 22–4; cognitive creation of

INDEX

consequences 17–18; cognitive creation of reality 16–17; cognitive-philosophic cure 18–22; human cognition 12–16; primacy of thinking 11–12

paradigms 15
passion xii–xiii, 25–33; creating passionate purpose 33–44
passionate purpose 161
Patti 28
Paula 97
Perceptual Beliefs 24n4
perfectionism xiii, 137–48; arguments against 149–54
Perfectionistic Demanding 24n5
personal responsibility xiii, 91–105
Perspective 24n5
Phil 147
PITA (Pain In The Ass) 101
power of passionate purpose xii–xiii, 25–33; creating, 33–44
Practical Preferring 24n5
premeditated acceptance and forgiveness, Interpersonal Intelligence 60–4
primacy of thinking 11–12
process of REBT 85
procrastination 145
psychological freedom xiii, 107–21
PTSD 123–32
purpose 32; creating 40–1; happiness 155–68; living 42–4; reflecting on 33–9
pursuit of elegance xiii, 123–31

Rachel 10
Rational Emotive Behavior Therapy (REBT) 4, 7–9, 24n1, 24n5, 108
rational thought 161
reality: cognitive creation of reality 16–17; perfectionism, 150
REBT (Rational Emotive Behavior Therapy) 4, 7–9, 24n1, 24n5; process 85, 108

reflecting on purpose 33–9
responsibility, personal responsibility 91–105
Robert 97
Roosevelt, Theodore 91
Russ 79–85

Sabrina 45–50, 52
Sam 75
Samuel 134
Sara 134
Sartre, Jean-Paul 81
Schneider, Jack 140–1
Scott 146–7
Self 82–5
Self-Acceptance 24n5
self-damning 102
Self-Damning Depression 49, 146; USA (Unconditional Self-Acceptance) 89–90
self-discipline 161
self-esteem xiii, 75–90, 84, 87–9
Self-Rating 24n5
shame 147
Shelly 123–32, 135
Shirley 10
splitting 113
St. Augustine 120
Stephen 97
Stocker, Bill 39
Susan 133

Ted 134
Thucydides 107
Toni 111–15, 120
trust 46–7, 57–9, 73
trying 99
unconditional personal responsibility xiii, 91–105
Unconditional Self-Acceptance (USA), 84, 89–90

Vic 147

well-being, destroying 86–7